D0048829

GREAT DOG STORIES

Heartwarming Tales of Remarkable Dogs

ROXANNE WILLEMS SNOPEK

VICTORIA · VANCOUVER · CALGARY

Copyright © 2011 Roxanne Willems Snopek

All rights reserved. No part of this publication may be reproduced, stored in a retrieval system or transmitted in any form or by any means—electronic, mechanical, audio recording or otherwise—without the written permission of the publisher or a photocopying licence from Access Copyright, Toronto, Canada.

Heritage House Publishing Company Ltd.
www.heritagehouse.ca

Library and Archives Canada Cataloguing in Publication
Snopek, Roxanne Willems
Great dog stories: heartwarming tales of remarkable dogs /Roxanne Willems Snopek.

(Amazing stories)
Issued also in electronic format.
ISBN 978-1-926613-97-0

1. Working dogs—Anecdotes. 2. Human-animal relationships—Anecdotes. I. Title. II. Series: Amazing stories (Victoria, B.C.)

SF428.2.S56   2011 636.73   C2011-904689-X

Series editor: Lesley Reynolds.
Cover design: Chyla Cardinal. Interior design: Frances Hunter.
Cover photo: Nevin Giesbrecht Photography/iStockphoto.
Chapter 11, "The Gift of Courage," originally appeared in *Chicken Soup for the Pet Lover's Soul*, Health Communications Inc., 1998, and appears in this book in altered form.

The interior of this book was printed on 100% post-consumer recycled paper, processed chlorine free and printed with vegetable-based inks.

Heritage House acknowledges the financial support for its publishing program from the Government of Canada through the Canada Book Fund (CBF), Canada Council for the Arts and the province of British Columbia through the British Columbia Arts Council and the Book Publishing Tax Credit.

14 13 12 11   1 2 3 4 5
Printed in Canada

To Molly, our retired racing greyhound,
who hasn't done a single useful thing
since the day we got her—except love us.

Contents

Prologue

LEEANN O'REILLY GLANCED THROUGH THE woods into the late autumn sky. Daylight was fading, and a dense chill was settling in the Newfoundland air. It was time to head back.

"Dakota!" she called. "Max!"

She searched the forest for a pair of friendly shadows ambling through the bush, but her Rottweilers were nowhere in sight. LeeAnn took a few tentative steps into the woods, and then she heard it: the telltale jingle—the bells she had fastened to her dogs' collars to warn away wild animals. But the sound grew fainter even as she walked toward it. Again, she called for the dogs, an edge of annoyance in her voice now. This time they burst out of the trees, muscles rippling and tongues lolling as they flung themselves on her. They rubbed their massive heads against her legs and she broke into a laugh. "Forgiven," she murmured fondly.

Then, as suddenly as they had arrived, the dogs tensed. Pulling away, they stood swivelling their ears, their noses lifted to the wind. A long, low growl rolled from Dakota's throat and her hackles rose. Max froze, his attention trained on a clump of bush ahead, his body poised to leap. LeeAnn could see no sign of danger, but she felt the terror rise deep in her belly.

As the snarls of the dogs began to build, LeeAnn took stock. She had no weapons, no phone and no radio. She had nowhere to hide. Max gave a single, short bark and it happened: the woods exploded with the fury of a beast enraged.

Only her two Rottweilers stood between LeeAnn and the black bull moose charging straight for her.

CHAPTER

1

On Centre Stage

FROM BIRTH, JAMMIE WAS DESTINED to be a star. Her bright eyes, elegant bone structure, luscious coat and regal bearing all pointed to a career in that competitive world of canine beauty contests: the show ring. Indeed, before her first birthday, Jammie (pronounced Jay-me) was a titled conformation champion, beautifully exhibiting the sought-after traits of the ideal silky terrier. She had already lived up to her distinguished registered name, Champion Kedwell's Silk Pajamas.

But success didn't sit well with Jammie. When campaigning for titles, dogs and their owners might spend every weekend on the road, travelling to shows. They meet with hundreds of strangers in new surroundings filled with unfamiliar sights, sounds and smells. On the judging table, dogs must stand calmly while strangers handle them. If necessary, judges will touch every part of the dog's body.

It got to be too much for Jammie. Her owner, Ros Scott of London, Ontario, watched her dog's happy personality gradually give way to anxiety. Jammie began avoiding strangers. In competition, she would watch the judges over her shoulder, her eyes narrowed in suspicion. Worst of all, she grew suspicious of children. As a result, Ros had to find ways to keep children from touching Jammie unexpectedly. She did what she could, hoping the problem was temporary. But Jammie became more and more anxious and unpredictable around strangers—to the point of growling and snapping if approached by surprise. With great reluctance, Ros admitted that although her dog was a stunning example of the silky terrier physique, Jammie's temperament was less than ideal. Jammie had an aggression problem.

Ros Scott had problems of her own. A decade earlier, she'd had surgery to fuse two vertebrae in her lumbar spine. Now she was beginning to experience pain in her hip. But Ros ignored her increasing discomfort and redoubled her efforts to quell Jammie's anxieties. Ros took the terrier out of the show ring and began agility training—an activity involving a demanding obstacle course run by both dog and handler. It was just what Jammie needed; she was challenged both physically and mentally, but her exposure to strangers was greatly reduced. Within a year, Jammie achieved her Canadian Kennel Club Novice Agility title.

With the title under their belts, Ros sought new challenges. She had always toyed with the idea of trying musical freestyle, a type of obedience-dance competition often compared to pairs figure skating.

Music has long been a part of dog training; in obedience classes, it adds an element of fun to the task of perfecting rhythmic pace. Obedience drill-team demonstrations are often performed to music. But musical freestyle obedience only began to emerge as a sport in its own right in the late 1980s. Inspired by the musical routines of equine dressage, demonstrations of this new dog sport began to pop up at various dog shows across the United Kingdom and North America. Since that time, the sport has exploded in popularity. Audiences and competitors alike thrill over the delight the dogs take in performing their routines and over the vivid evidence of the bonds dogs share with their owners.

Ros thought that musical freestyle obedience, like agility, might be another way to help Jammie overcome her anxiety. Ros hoped she could find something they both enjoyed that she could manage in spite of her diminishing mobility. So, in January 2002, Ros drove with Jammie to a workshop in Michigan. There, they discovered that not only was the event a lot of fun, but that they were considerably better than Ros had expected. In order to compete, however, they had a lot of work to do. The best-case scenario for success in the sport of

musical freestyle obedience involves two things: a tempera-
mentally well-adjusted dog who loves to work (preferably a
border collie) and an athletic owner (preferably 20 to 30 years
old) with a background in dance. Ros and Jammie didn't fit
these criteria. But Ros still wanted to give it a try, and she and
Jammie started to develop their routine.

Ros quickly learned that this activity was no easier on
her back than agility. Her body began to protest in earnest,
and after one lengthy road trip to Denver for another workshop, she arrived at the hotel barely able to walk. She began
to use a wheelchair whenever possible to save her energy for
demonstrations. In spite of anti-inflammatories and pain-
killers, some days the back pain was barely tolerable.

Still, nothing ever came between her and the terrier. Ros
soon realized, in fact, that their bond had become stronger
and more intuitive than ever. Jammie seemed to know when
her dance partner was in pain. It shouldn't have been a surprise; musical freestyle relies heavily on unspoken signals
such as body language and facial expression. Dogs and handlers work in sync, constantly adapting to the slightest change
in each other's movements. On the days when Ros wasn't able
to move as freely, Jammie moved more, compensating for her
partner and drawing the eyes of their audience onto herself.

Ros's health continued to deteriorate rapidly until she
was using a wheelchair constantly at home. In addition to
the medications, she began getting regular massage therapy, but still the pain increased. In an attempt to help her

understand the seriousness of her condition, the therapist explained to Ros what was happening in her body: the muscles in her legs had shortened and rotated, pulling her spine out of alignment. Sitting only made the pain worse. Carefully chosen activity would help, but she had to start gradually. Most likely, the sudden immersion into agility was what had started the domino effect of damage.

So Ros began focusing on the demanding and sometimes excruciating work of rehabilitating and strengthening her muscles and also continued to practise the musical freestyle routines she loved to do with Jammie. It was a difficult time for Ros. Inadvertent contact with a sensitive spot sometimes brought such intense pain it nearly made her pass out. Jammie learned to accommodate her partner even more, picking up on the subtle changes in movement dictated by discomfort and moving carefully to avoid hurting her. As a result, their performance got even better.

Ros and Jammie began to compete. Ros will never forget their performance at the first World Canine Freestyle Organization event in May 2002. The crowd fell silent as the pair entered the ring. They took their spots and stood poised, eyes locked on each other, listening for the music. For a moment, the air hung hushed and expectant, and the music began. With a leap, the little dog came to life, rolling, twirling and jumping, stepping backward and forward, executing a series of intricate moves in perfect harmony with her human partner. It all fit into a perfectly choreographed pattern that, by the end of the performance, brought everyone in the audience to their feet. Ros Scott and her silky terrier Champion Kedwell's Silk Pajamas had made magic once more. They took their bows and walked to the edge of the ring. Ros immediately reached for her wheelchair and dropped into it, exhausted. Jammie leaped up and settled into her owner's lap, panting happily. When the judges tallied up their marks, success overshadowed pain. Ros and Jammie placed first in the beginners' class, receiving high marks for both technical merit and artistic impression.

Later that year, Ros met with a surgeon again to discuss fusing two more vertebrae. It needed to be done, but the surgeon explained that until her muscles had developed greater strength and flexibility, the operation was destined to fail. Ros had a lot of work ahead of her.

The harder Ros worked, the harder Jammie worked. Soon, the awards were piling up. Jammie received her Agility Dog Canada title, points toward her Beginners Musical Freestyle title, and even a trophy for the highest scoring toy dog in musical freestyle. Jammie just wouldn't quit.

In fact, now she leads. "She doesn't always want to follow the practised routine," says Ros with a laugh. "If she goes from plan A to plan B, you have to go with the flow and keep smiling. No one else knows if she does three spins instead of two."

Ros admits to being apprehensive before each performance, wondering each time what new thing her dog will try, but Jammie clearly knows what she's doing. She's good at it because she loves it and has become a star. If Jammie recognizes a song on the radio, she has been known to jump off the couch and dive into her routine. Ros has even caught Jammie twirling in front of the mirror! Like many dogs, she hates having her feet touched; it's a fight to the finish to get her nails trimmed. But get out the nail polish and the story changes. Jammie loves having sparkly gold nails, and she sits calmly for her manicure, like any good diva.

She recognizes "her" music, but Ros knows better than to use a certain song too long. Jammie needs variety, and if she becomes bored with a routine, her moves show it. She rolls her eyes, and Ros can imagine her thoughts: "Oh for Pete's sake. Not this one again!"

Jammie might be a star but she also seems to understand that stardom demands professional behaviour. When Ros pulls out the frilly collar that indicates it's "show time," Jammie tucks all her anxieties away. The little dog knows that she must tolerate a certain amount of adoration from her fans, and she is especially aware of people with mental disabilities, allowing them to hug and pet her. Where she once might have snarled or snapped, she now accepts the attention calmly, if not enthusiastically. To her, it's a small price to pay for success.

Just as Jammie has learned to read Ros, Ros has learned to work around Jammie's sensitivities. Kids still find the little dog irresistible and, tired of body-blocking hordes of affectionate pint-sized fans, Ros came up with a couple of ways around it.

"I tell them she doesn't like to be touched, but she'll do a trick for them," says Ros. Now, when a child approaches, Jammie immediately starts spinning. She's also learned to "say hello" to children: she runs up to them, licks their hands and then returns to Ros for a treat. For most kids— and for Jammie—it's an acceptable compromise.

But Ros knows better than to push it. By a hundred tiny signals, she can tell when Jammie has reached her limit. The tension in her back, the tilt of her head, the set of her ears all give clues to her comfort level. Ros particularly notes how aggressively Jammie takes her treat. "When she snaps it out of my hand," she says, "I know her stress level is getting too high."

Ros and Jammie are so attuned to each other, it some- times seems like they can read each other's minds. Perhaps this is part of the magic that makes them such a success- ful team. "When we're dancing," Ros says, "Jammie's eyes lock with mine. She grins at me. I grin at her. It's like we're lovers dancing together." Audiences and judges alike melt in the face of such a relationship. Among Ros's most trea- sured awards are several trophies for most bonded dog and handler.

By all accounts, the duo shouldn't be successful in dog sports: a 50-year-old woman with mobility problems and a toy dog with aggression problems. But by accepting their limitations and working together, they've both achieved more than most of their competitors. Just recently, the pair received the coveted High in Trial title in an agility competition in Andover, Massachusetts. Ros could choose to compete in handicapped divisions, but she doesn't want to. She doesn't need to. She'll always have to be careful with her back, even though her fitness has improved enough to allow her to exchange the wheelchair for a cane. Surgery will help, but only to a certain extent. Ros knows this. She also knows that unless she challenges herself, she'll never know what she can accomplish.

And she's quick to give the credit to Jammie. "It's all due to a dog who gives her heart and soul."

2

On the Force

EVERYONE KNOWS THAT NO CRIME can be solved without evidence linking the suspect to the event. Naturally, suspects go to great lengths to dispose of such evidence, but there's one thing they can never remove: their scent.

In Maple Ridge, British Columbia, during the spring of 1995, Corporal Rick Chaulk and his canine partner, Police Service Dog Jake, were called to assist in solving a horrific crime. The body of a man had been discovered, stabbed and beaten to death the previous night. Investigators at the scene quickly identified two suspects.

"They called me to do a search because they hadn't found a murder weapon or any other related evidence," says Chaulk. He knew that the chance of finding clues was best while the trail was fresh. Human beings are constantly shedding scent particles, leaving an invisible cone-shaped olfactory trail marking their movements. The particles hover in the air like dust before settling on the ground and eventually disappearing. A brisk wind can disturb the trail, as can rain, snow or the overlay of other scents. So Chaulk and Jake wasted no time combing through the residential neighbourhood where the murder had occurred, looking for any evidence that might help them solve the crime. Systematically, inch by inch, the pair went over a three-block area near the victim's home.

"The first day turned up nothing related to the crime," says Chaulk. "So we came back the next day and expanded the search area to a one-square-block radius of the crime scene." They'd worked their way over most of this larger area when Jake suddenly picked up something. He began moving back and forth, narrowing the trail down, looking for the strongest source of the scent. About seven houses away from the victim's home, he began to whine in excitement, sniffing furiously until he reached a hedge. It was clear to Chaulk that Jake had found something with human scent on it. "You learn to read your dog," explains Chaulk. "You look for body language. When Jake indicates, he becomes very animated: his tail starts wagging, he tries to get at the article."

Something lay hidden deep in the hedge, and Jake was determined to get at it. Chaulk quickly climbed into the hedge too, trying to see what Jake was so excited about. He also needed to make sure that if they had found something important, Jake wouldn't contaminate it. Chaulk peered through the thicket and then saw it: a baseball bat.

During training sessions, the dogs are rewarded in a variety of ways. They always receive enthusiastic praise from their human partner. Sometimes they get a brief play session with a favourite toy. Occasionally, they get to play with the search object itself. During a real evidence search, however, the handler tries to keep the dog away from the article for fear he will destroy some vital clue. Jake worked solely for Chaulk's approval, and Chaulk piled it on. "Atta-boy, Jake! Good boy!"

But Jake was a new dog, barely out of training. In fact, this was his first official search. How would Jake know the difference between a baseball bat used in a crime two days ago and one lost by schoolboys the previous summer? "Human scent evaporates in time," explains Chaulk. "Jake's indication was so strong I knew the bat had been recently deposited there." And, as a new dog, Jake would be less likely to pick up an old scent. Experienced dogs can learn to distinguish "cold" trails, but Chaulk knew that Jake wasn't likely to do this. Whoever had stuffed this bat into the hedge had done it recently.

They'd made good progress, but more work had to be done and the clock was ticking. Police surveillance noted that the two suspects had been seen walking along the railroad tracks near the Fraser River under the cover of night.

They appeared to be carrying something, but it was too dark to see what it was. When the pair left the area a short time later, they were empty-handed, so Chaulk and Jake went in to see what they could find. By this time, the light was quickly fading, but the canine sense of smell is so much more powerful than sight that nightfall makes little difference. Jake searched off leash under bushes, behind trees and up and down the railroad tracks, while Chaulk stumbled along behind, flashlight in hand, hoping his dog knew what he was doing.

After only a few minutes, Jake began to focus on a gravel area near the tracks. Again, he pawed and dug until his quarry was revealed. When Chaulk caught up, he pulled Jake back to look for himself and saw, glinting through the gravel, the tip of a gun. Jake was on a roll. He'd found a missing pair of rifles.

Instinct is a strange thing, and Corporal Chaulk's instincts told him they weren't finished yet. "A gut feeling told me we should be thorough, and I just figured there was more to it than that," he recalls. Although no official order had sent them out, five days after the murder he and Jake did a "speculative search." They went back to the river, had a good run and then made their way back to where they'd found the guns. "Search!" Chaulk commanded. Instantly, Jake went to work, searching back and forth over the rough ground, collecting information and looking for the particular scents that identified the suspects.

Jake reached a clearing, and again his head went up and his tail started beating the rhythm of success. His find? A stained pair of old blue sweatpants. Chaulk praised Jake, but privately he doubted that the item had any value. Many people used these trails, after all, and they were a favourite place for late-night parties. Who knew by what dubious means those pants had gotten there?

Nevertheless, procedure dictated that the forensic team be called in to retrieve the garment for preservation and analysis. While Chaulk impatiently awaited their arrival, he asked Jake to search one last time, just in case. Within minutes, Jake began to dig beneath a nearby stump. Chaulk ran to check the area himself. "I pushed the dirt with my foot and that's when a knife was exposed," he says.

Chaulk didn't know it at the time, but the last piece of the puzzle had just fallen into place. Jake had uncovered the knife that was used to stab the victim. Forensic tests later revealed that the stains on the sweatpants were the blood of the murder victim. They had everything they needed to build a strong case against the two suspects. The sweatpants belonged to one of the suspects and had been worn during the killing. The victim had been killed by a blow to the head, stabbed and robbed. Without the meticulous work of Corporal Chaulk and his canine partner, Police Service Dog Jake, the offenders might have gone unpunished. Instead, both men were convicted of the crime and sentenced to time in prison.

Jake's career was launched, inaugurating a brilliant partnership that would continue until his retirement at the age of eight. Chaulk still works as a police dog handler, but no dog will ever fully replace Jake. "I raised Jake from an eight-week-old puppy," he remembers. Chaulk did all the necessary pre-training to prepare Jake for the formal work at the RCMP Police Dog Service Training Centre in Innisfail, Alberta. For six years, Jake and Chaulk were barely separated, working together and living together. But then came the moment when something changed, and Chaulk knew his partner had had enough. "It was a tough call because he was still working fine," says Chaulk, "but you could see it in his eyes. He was tired."

Chaulk knew that retiring Jake meant losing him. Although breaking their partnership was devastating, he knew only a complete separation would give Jake the best opportunity to enjoy his old age. Retired police dogs rarely stay with their handlers, unless the handler also retires from the dog unit. "These dogs live to work," Chaulk says. "If I kept him but every morning walked past him with a new dog on our way to work, while he stayed home in the kennel, it would kill him." Instead, Chaulk made the agonizing decision to say goodbye while Jake was still young and healthy enough to enjoy a few years of ordinary life. "It only takes that one call that maybe finishes their career or ruins their health," he adds. He didn't want to take that chance with Jake.

Chaulk handpicked a family who he knew would give his partner the retirement he'd earned, and while he hears about Jake occasionally, he's never visited him. It took Jake a few months to adjust, but he's happy now in his new home, and Chaulk doesn't want to remind him of their old life together. It would be too hard on both of them.

"Jake worked hard," he says. "I told him 'go be a dog, eat table scraps and lie by the fire. You deserve it.' But it's tough."

* * *

The danger of police service-dog work takes many different forms. One night in November of 1978, in the Fraser Valley, a reckless driving complaint was called in—a deceptively innocuous call. Police officers attempted to apprehend the driver, but he fled in a high-speed chase, finally screeching to a stop in front of a house where a large, raucous party was in progress. He leapt out of his car and disappeared into the woods behind the house. RCMP corporal Terry Barter of Chilliwack, British Columbia, and Police Service Dog Major were called in with the request to "apprehend as many suspects as possible."

Major quickly identified the trail of the driver, found him and brought him down. But while Corporal Barter was handcuffing the man, several hostile-looking young men suddenly appeared. "When we caught our guy, he started screaming, attracting people from the party," says Barter. Two men jumped Barter from behind, and someone else boot-kicked Major viciously in the side, hard enough that a veterinary examination later revealed a ruptured spleen. Not knowing who had kicked him, Major reacted by biting the suspect on the ground. The suspect began screaming again, and his companions escalated their attack. Fearing for Major's life, Barter pulled him out of the fray and locked him in the police car.

Other police officers quickly helped subdue the group, but as the officers returned to their vehicles, more young people poured out of the house, shouting taunts and threats. "At one point we had about 50 to 80 people outside chanting 'kill the pigs, kill the pigs,'" says Barter.

The driver and two other men were taken into custody and charged with assaulting a peace officer. One of them, the one who had kicked Major, vented his fury in a particularly ominous way: "I know where you live!" he shouted at Barter. "I'm coming to kill the dog!" Unfortunately, when the young man was released early the next morning, the first item on his agenda was revenge—and he wasted no time. At 6:19 a.m., Barter heard the crunch of tires near his house. Major was resting safely inside instead of in his kennel in the yard, but no one else knew this. While Barter was hurriedly pulling on some clothes, he heard voices outside calling for the dog, and he realized that the young man and his friend were trying to get Major to reveal himself. "I knew why they were there," he says. "I was prepared to defend my residence if they got out of the vehicle armed."

But something spooked them. Just as Barter went outside, the truck roared away. Moments later, five shotgun blasts exploded through the morning air. Barter suspected they'd be back, and he was right. Later that day, neighbours reported the same truck lurking near Barter's home. This time, police nailed the young man before he could get away. Major was safe again. For now. But the unsettling incident reminded Barter that every job he and Major tackled could be the last. And a year earlier, it almost had been.

One spring morning in 1977, a prisoner from Agassiz Mountain Prison (now Mountain Institution) escaped during a fishing trip on British Columbia's Fraser River. Barter and Major were brought to the location where the prisoner had last been seen, a wooded area near the riverbank. The prisoner had chosen his path deliberately, travelling over rocky ground that was the least likely to carry tracks and the most difficult to follow. He'd taken weather, daylight and terrain into account and had probably thought he had a good chance of escaping successfully. Indeed, he might very well have been successful if it hadn't been for Major.

By that time, Barter and Major had been partners on the RCMP dog unit for about six years. They had gone into every kind of situation, from avalanche rescue, missing-person searches and body recovery to chasing escaped convicts. This was nothing new.

Major immediately picked up the prisoner's scent and started straining at the leash, eager to begin pursuit over the rough, mountainous terrain. Police dogs normally work on a long tracking leash, but about two-thirds of the way into the chase, the grade angled up sharply, and Barter knew that Major needed his freedom. Barter himself needed both hands to navigate the incline, which by then exceeded 50 degrees. Plus, he had another worry: in the back of his mind nagged the thought that they might need to defend themselves against an ambush from above.

Major leapt ahead, scrambling over the rocky terrain, and the officer hoped his dog's strength and agility were equal to the task at hand. Then, through the brush and rocky outcroppings in front of him, Barter heard the unmistakable sound of slipping shale, followed by a heavy thud, a yelp and then silence. Barter hurried over the jagged ground, frantic to catch up with his dog. When he reached him, he saw that Major had taken a nasty fall. Major looked shaken, but when Barter ran his hands quickly over the dog, he could find no obvious injuries. He hoped that Major's thick coat had protected him from the worst of the biting rocks.

Barter felt sure they were close on the heels of their quarry, but now he worried that his partner had been injured. Major hid any signs of pain, however, and clearly had no intention of quitting, so they continued upward.

About 60 metres below the snow line, Major turned abruptly, crossing a field and doubling back into the woods. He was on to something! Barter rushed to where he found the dog standing, excitedly indicating his find: a carefully hidden cache of three tobacco tins, a book and a box of biscuits. Barter put the items in a safe place for recovery later on, and they continued the hunt. Once again the track angled sharply upwards, and as Major bounded ahead, Barter lost sight of him.

Suddenly, he heard the dog cry out again, but this time something was different. Instinctively, Barter knew that Major had cornered the convict, which meant the dog was in danger. Barter scrambled toward the sound, shouting for Major to return. Finally, as he crested the ridge, he caught a glimpse of the prisoner disappearing into the woods. But where was Major? Barter scanned the area frantically, but when he caught sight of his dog, it wasn't relief he felt. Major staggered toward him, trying desperately to obey the recall command, his chest and shoulders covered with blood. Before he made it back to his handler, he stumbled and collapsed. As Barter rushed to his dog's side, Major suddenly heaved himself up again to go after the prisoner. Barter hadn't had a chance to see the wound, but he guessed his dog had been stabbed, probably deeply, judging from the blood loss. The officer commanded him to return. Major ignored the command.

All Corporal Barter could do was follow the trail of blood and hope he reached his dog in time. He braced himself for the worst, but when he burst through the trees into a small clearing, nothing could have prepared him for the sight ahead. On the ground lay the prisoner, terrified but unharmed, with a snarling, blood-soaked Major standing guard over him.

The pursuit was over, but now Barter was faced with a desperate escapee armed with an unknown weapon and a police dog rapidly going into shock from blood loss. Barter needed to get the prisoner disarmed and restrained, but what he wanted to do was attend to his dog. As the corporal reached for his handcuffs, the prisoner lunged into his bag. Instantly, Barter knew what he had to do: he shot the prisoner in the leg.

The next 15 minutes before backup arrived seemed to stretch on endlessly, the wait punctuated by the moans of the injured prisoner and Major's shallow breathing. Later, Barter would face a harsh reprimand for shooting the prisoner in his care, but in those moments, Barter's only concern was for his canine partner. He knew the prisoner was not in danger of dying from his injury, but Major, who was growing weaker by the moment, might very well be. Barter packed the gaping wound in Major's neck as well as he could; all that remained was to wait for the helicopter and pray that his dog would survive. The distant sound of helicopter blades was never more welcome!

But where does a helicopter land on a mountain? "We had to walk more than a kilometre to where the helicopter could hover over a large rock," recalls Barter. Both Major and the prisoner had to be loaded into the aircraft while it hung in mid-air, officers pushing and pulling them into position as best they could. When they finally left the bush and made it back into town, Barter rushed Major to the veterinary hospital, where an examination revealed a nine-centimetre-deep stab wound that had severed the dog's jugular vein and a large nerve in his throat. Major had suffered severe blood loss. In a two-hour surgical procedure, the veterinary team did the best they could, but they weren't optimistic. "They told me to take him home to die," recalls Barter. But the corporal crossed his fingers. Only an incredibly strong, determined dog would complete his task in spite of life-threatening injury. Barter clung to the idea that if Major was strong enough to corner the prisoner, he was strong enough to pull through his injury.

And he did. Day by day, Major regained more strength until Barter knew that, amazingly, he was going to recover. "They kept testing him for nerve damage, but they never found any," adds Barter. Exactly two weeks after the event, Major was reinstated to full, active duty. He'd learned something important about knives, though, a lesson he never forgot. "He was always careful about suspects on the ground after that," says Barter. "He was only going to be stabbed once."

Major lived with Barter and his family for his entire adult life. As tough as he was with criminals, Major was overwhelmingly patient and gentle with children. Both of Barter's newborn children were brought home from the hospital in the police cruiser, car seats belted alongside

Major. At one point, the family's yard was unfenced except for Major's large dog run, so when Barter's little daughter wanted to play outside, they let her toddle around after Major inside the run. No playground could be more secure, and she clearly loved it, perhaps too much. "Our daughter started to bark along with Major," Barter laughs.

Major would have retired with Barter, but cancer cut his life short just before his 10th birthday. He worked right up until the morning of his death.

Corporal Barter knows that his job is risky. It's fraught with frustration, and the rewards can be few and far between. But the bond he shares with his canine partners means everything to him. "I joined the RCMP to be a dog handler," he says. "I stayed at this job because it's what I wanted to do."

Faith, Hope and Healing

FOR MOST OF HER ADULT LIFE, Heather MacLeod of Fredericton, New Brunswick, has been heavily involved in dog sports, competing with her German shepherd Bailey in conformation shows, obedience and tracking. Bailey's successes have made history in the German shepherd world: in 1998, she became the first white German shepherd to earn a Tracking Dog Excellent title in both Canada and the United States. But it was her win in the conformation ring that really threw people for a loop. "White shepherds," Heather explains, "are sort of the 'black sheep' of the German shepherd breed."

When Bailey was about three years old, a good age to have puppies, Heather began making tentative plans to breed her. She knew exactly which male she wanted for the father, but he lived in Michigan. The logistics of timing and travel were complicated, and the window of opportunity during which a dog can become pregnant is only open a short time—twice each year. Heather didn't want to put Bailey through the stress of being shipped out to where the male lived, so she briefly considered artificial insemination. "Males are hardly ever shipped, but semen can be," she explains. "But that is very costly, and the success rate isn't as high as with a natural breeding." She resigned herself to a long puppyless wait. It wasn't entirely hopeless; the male was being actively campaigned on the show circuit, so there was a chance they'd be able to meet. But Heather didn't get her hopes up.

Then, out of the blue, she was contacted with the news: the male she liked was going to be competing in a nearby show right during the time Heather expected Bailey to be in season. Was she still interested in getting them together?

She certainly was, and the romance was duly arranged and consummated. On December 10, 1998, Bailey gave birth to the much-anticipated litter of puppies, including one that Heather would later keep. Heather was ecstatic. The puppies were every bit as beautiful as she'd hoped, and Bailey appeared to be enjoying her pampered status as a new mother.

But the joy was short-lived. On December 11, Heather received a phone call that brought her abruptly down to earth and signalled the beginning of her own private nightmare. It was her doctor, calling with the results of some laboratory tests she'd had recently after complaining of a persistent cough. The chest X-ray indicated that she had a mass in her lung. A naturally healthy, optimistic person, Heather struggled numbly to make sense of the news. The doctors couldn't say what the mass was or what it would mean for her. Until further tests were done, she'd simply have to hope for the best. Heather continued to care for Bailey and the puppies, but it was hard to think of the future. She was scheduled for surgery.

The pups were four weeks old in January 1999 when Heather went into surgery to have the mass removed. She had been warned ahead of time that she could lose part or all of her lung in the procedure. When Heather was rolled into the operating theatre that day, she had no idea what kind of news she'd wake up to, but it didn't take long to find out. The mass and a lobe of her lung were removed and sent to the pathology lab for tests. The results were clear: Heather had Hodgkin's lymphoma. Her doctors, however, were cautiously optimistic; as cancers go, this one has a relatively high cure rate.

The tumour itself had been successfully removed, but Heather would need chemotherapy to destroy any cancer cells still circulating in her lymphatic system. Heather assimilated all the information she could find about her condition while trying to keep the fear at bay. As soon as she recovered sufficiently from her surgery, she began the first course of chemotherapy.

Throughout the ordeal, Bailey's puppies continued to grow fatter and more rambunctious until, in February, they were old enough to go to their new homes. By this time, Heather had decided she would keep one for herself; she named her puppy Faith.

It was a challenging time in her life to have a puppy, and Heather hoped she knew what she was doing. Her experience in dog sports, particularly the tracking she and Bailey loved, was something she thought might help her through this difficult time. But dog sports are physically demanding, and she had a long way to go in her recovery. Six months of chemotherapy had sapped her energy, and only a few months after her last round, she was devastated to learn that it hadn't achieved what they'd hoped for. Her lymphoma was back. Heather faced a difficult decision, but ultimately there was no choice to be made.

At the end of 1999, when everyone else around her was preparing to celebrate the coming of the new millennium, Heather was in the hospital again, sequestered in the isolation ward. In a world full of champagne-toasting revellers, one woman struggled to keep down popsicles and wondered if she'd still be around to celebrate next year. Before the advent of the New Year, Heather would receive a stronger form of high-dose chemotherapy, followed by a bone-marrow transplant.

At this high intensity, the chemotherapy destroys all fast-growing cells. It's a kind of last-ditch, scorched-earth strategy. Cancer cells are wiped out, but vital red and white blood cells, platelets and stem cells are obliterated along with them. "Essentially," explains Heather, "they kill your immune system with the high-dose chemo, as a sort of collateral damage, and then they 'rescue' you with the bone marrow transplant."

Heather remained isolated in the hospital until mid-January 2000, while her body fought to rebuild its immune system. This time, the treatment worked, but the roller-coaster ride wasn't over yet. Heather had one last trial to overcome. The chronic exhaustion that accompanies bone-marrow transplant recovery left her unable to do more than the simplest tasks. When she finally came home, although she was anxious to work with Bailey again and start training Faith, she could do very little. Frustrated at times, she struggled to be patient, reminding herself that this was a normal part of the process. "I try very hard not to make people afraid of chemo," she emphasizes. "Chemo saved my life. It was no picnic but I'd do it all over again, no question."

Then spring rolled around, bringing with it a hint of her old energy. "By the end of March, I was growing some hair back and feeling almost human," she recalls. "I'd had my 38th birthday and wished to have a few more!" The future beckoned. It was time to push herself, force her body and mind to recover. She even set herself a goal: that fall, she intended to take the American Tracking Dog test with Faith. She didn't know if the puppy would be ready, but all she could do was try.

She started by taking Faith out into the field on very short beginner tracking exercises. Gradually, as her condition improved and Faith became more competent, Heather laid longer scent tracks for the pup to follow. In the early days, she would sometimes stay out for only a few minutes at a time, but that's all Faith needed. "It fit in so well with my recovery," says Heather. "I told people 'tracking with her is my therapy. It's getting me better!'"

From her past involvement in pet visitation with Bailey, Heather knew about the many positive effects animals have on hospital and nursing-home patients. Now she intended to reap the benefits of animal-assisted therapy herself, as much as possible. She continued tracking with Faith in the field that summer, determined to meet her goal of taking the test in September. Their performance was beside the point; rather, Heather focused on doing the work and making progress.

That fall, they were as ready as they could be. Heather crossed her fingers and they took the test. Faith passed. "I was thrilled!" she remembers. "I can't even explain the feeling when we passed the test. I thought 'That's it, we're back, baby!'" Their success continued into the following month, when Faith got her Canadian Tracking Dog title.

For Heather, 2000 was "the year back from hell." The physical challenges were tremendous, but the ordeal of riding such emotional highs and lows was at least as difficult. Without the tasks associated with the sport of tracking and the joy she gets from it, Heather doubts she'd have coped so well. "A major part of my recovery was the work with my dogs. I do so much with them! That's why it was so important when I hit that first title with Faith. I felt like I was back in the world of the living again."

The three-year mark is the point at which a person is considered cured of Hodgkin's lymphoma. "I just had my three-year checkup and I'm all clear," Heather reports with quiet joy.

Life was almost back to normal for Heather and her family. She continued working with the dogs and challenging them with new things: obedience, advanced tracking and agility, which Faith loves. "She's fast but I'm not!" laughs Heather. "The chemo actually damaged what's left of my lungs, so I get out of breath really quickly." In May 2003, Bailey, who was spayed after her second litter, earned both her Flyball Dog and her Flyball Dog Excellent titles. "She would really like to enter squirrel-chasing competitions," says Heather, "but I just can't find any, so she's settling for flyball instead." Flyball is a rapid-fire relay in which dogs run to a ball, trigger its release, catch the ball and race back with it to the next dog in line. Heather loved it almost as much as Bailey did.

Still, one thing was missing. During Heather's illness, her much-loved old cat, Buckwheat, died. Although she missed his company and wanted a kitten, the doctors advised her to wait for two years after her bone-marrow transplant. Because some cats carry an organism called toxoplasma that can be dangerous to immune-compromised people, they wanted to let her fully regain her health before taking any chances.

The month her two-year time limit was up, during the drive home from work, Heather's eye caught a flash of white moving at the side of the road. To her alarm, she saw a kitten stagger out of the brush, directly into the path of her car. She swerved to avoid hitting the animal, then pulled over and got out of her car to search for it. When she found the kitten, she quickly realized that the poor animal was practically frozen, weak and starving and that it seemed to have given up fighting for life. She gathered the fragile creature into her jacket, hoping it wasn't too late. "I didn't even want to pat her; she was just fur over bones," says Heather.

Heather raced to the local veterinary clinic, where she was told the kitten was severely malnourished, dehydrated and hypothermic. The young animal would need special care to survive, and without an owner, its chances were slim. Heather decided instantly: the kitten would come home with her. "I knew this kitten was a gift sent especially for me," she says. "Before I had her home, I had already named her: Hope."

Tiny Hope gives her new friend Faith a head butt—the feline version of a hug. HEATHER MACLEOD

Heather wondered how Hope would get along with Bailey and Faith, but soon realized her worries were needless. Not long after Hope's arrival, Heather watched Faith tenderly nuzzle the tiny animal, then stretch out on her side, exposing her flank. Although she'd never had puppies, Faith was a natural caregiver. It looked as though the big dog was playing wet-nurse to Hope. Then Heather looked again. Faith *was* nursing Hope! The kitten nosed into the soft fur of Faith's belly, while the dog lay there as if this were nothing out of the ordinary. Heather leaned down and gently squeezed one of Faith's nipples. Milk. Faith looked up at her as if to say, "What did you expect?"

Faith and Bailey had helped their beloved owner through a difficult health crisis. It was only natural that now Faith would nurture Hope, too.

4

In the Classroom

ON A BRIGHT SUNDAY MORNING in Coalhurst, Alberta, teacher Judith Snowdon sat at the sidelines of Perfect Pooches' obedience ring, holding her breath. In a moment, all eyes would be on her German shepherd, Tuxedo Rose. But Snowdon had no worries about that. Already titled in obedience, draft work, scent hurdling and agility, Rose had earned more degrees than most people ever would. Snowdon had no doubt that Rose would perform well once again. It was Rose's handler, a young student named Kathleen, who Snowdon was concerned about. This obedience match, an afternoon of fun for most participants, was the final culmination of a major school project for Kathleen, who was born with spina bifida.

Over the years, Rose had played a number of roles in her job as canine assistant to Snowdon, who is a teacher and counsellor at the junior high school in Blairmore, Alberta. The dog patiently modelled for art students, striking various poses while they scrambled to capture her graceful lines on paper. She also frequently accompanied Snowdon to her classes, where as part of the health curriculum, as many as 75 students at a time would practise the proper way to meet a new dog and learn what to do when approached by a stray.

Aside from health education, Snowdon taught humane education, a class in which students learned to interact and care for animals with compassion and empathy. Snowdon also instructed the basics of dog training: how to modify an animal's behaviour using the same methods employed by professional trainers. In Rose, Snowdon had the perfect visual aid to illustrate how and why animals enrich our lives. Students tried their newfound skills out on Rose and then went home to practise them on their own dogs, choosing specific tasks to teach. Young Kathleen, however, had neither a dog nor a project.

Kathleen's physical challenges meant she needed the aid of arm-brace crutches or her wheelchair to navigate the school's long hallways. Perhaps more difficult than her physical obstacles were the social and academic differences between her and the other students, differences that too often left Kathleen sitting apart from her classmates, on the outside looking in. Snowdon, however, had noticed that in the humane ed class the social barriers didn't seem as high. She hoped that an interesting and successful project might increase Kathleen's confidence and make it easier for her to connect with the other kids. But what, Snowdon wondered, could they assign that Kathleen could do?

"Can I use Rose for my project?" Kathleen asked Snowdon.

Snowdon hesitated. This was more participation than the dog was used to, and she might balk. Besides, what could Kathleen train Rose to do that the dog didn't already know? And how would the girl juggle a leash with her crutches? Then Snowdon had an idea: Rose had never specifically been taught to assist someone in a wheelchair. Perhaps Kathleen could train Rose to assist her with specific tasks—like pushing the handicap button to open doors—and to do it only when Kathleen was in her wheelchair instead of her braces. They formed a plan and got started.

Within a matter of days, Kathleen had taught Rose to retrieve dropped items and to open doors. But as their work progressed, the first snag in the plan became apparent: the two weren't bonded. Rose's attitude quickly deteriorated into, "Why should I do anything for you, kid?" And it was hard to blame her. Dog and wheelchair moved awkwardly side by side; on more than one occasion, Rose's tail got run over. Rose would yelp and run across the hall to Snowdon, and they'd have to start all over again.

Of course, as an experienced draft dog, Rose had no problem learning to tow Kathleen in her wheelchair. The problem, they quickly discovered, was getting her to stop! On their first attempt, Kathleen and Rose started down the hallway calmly enough, but as Rose saw the familiar door to Snowdon's office, her head pushed forward and her pace quickened. "Rose, slow down," begged Kathleen. But Rose was determined. Kathleen yanked and hauled on the harness, but to no avail. The girl braced herself as the chair crashed against the side of the door and they finally wobbled to a halt. It became a common routine, and students quickly learned to get out of the way when they saw the pair careening toward them.

There was another problem with towing the wheelchair, too. A split second after Rose would finally pull up, the chair would crash into her from behind. Rose would yelp, Kathleen would shriek and Snowdon would sigh. Snowdon's casual thought of having Rose assist a wheelchair-bound handler was turning out to be more of a hurdle than she expected.

"It took the better part of 12 weeks off and on for part of every day," says Judi. "During their practice sessions, I would see them heading down the hall, Kathleen holding on for dear life, brakes on, yelling 'Rose, easy, *Rose, easy!*' while Rose, her head down, her shoulders set, doggedly made her way to my office." It took time—and a lot of liver treats—but eventually the pair learned to travel together, safely and under control.

And the training had the unexpected benefit of raising

Kathleen's profile with the other students. She began to enjoy being noticed by her classmates. They started talking to her, asking how the assignment was progressing or teasing her good-heartedly about hearing her whiz past on another of her death-defying rides.

The dog and the student had overcome one hurdle, but had Kathleen been challenged enough? The other students in the class reported various problems in teaching their dogs at home. Rose already knew so much; in terms of training, Kathleen's work had been too easy. They needed to take it up a notch, and after a little thought, Judi came up with the perfect plan. A long-time obedience competitor herself, Judi assigned Kathleen the task of training Rose to complete all the necessary requirements for a leg toward an obedience title—with a wheelchair-bound handler. As part of the assignment, she gave Kathleen a copy of the Canadian Kennel Club rulebook for obedience competitions and told her to study it carefully. As Judi pointed out, Rose already knew the rules, but Kathleen had to learn them as well. Kathleen and Judi watched countless videotaped competitions, memorizing various moves and watching for the subtle details that can mean the difference between a passing mark and failure. Training to compete would be Kathleen's final project for humane education; as a bonus, studying the written rules would meet some of her English class requirements.

"I didn't cut her any slack," recalls Judi. "I told her, 'You said you were going to do this so you have to make it happen.'

When—and if—you get good enough, I'll tell you and you can go in a fun match.'" Then Judi added another incentive: she told Kathleen that if she and Rose entered, Judi herself would enter with another dog and compete against them. Judi knew Kathleen was motivated by the challenge, but worried how she might be affected by failure. After all, Judi was an accomplished trainer and competitor. "How will you feel about losing?" she asked Kathleen. "If I'm good enough to be there," answered Kathleen, "then that's good enough."

Kathleen redoubled her efforts. Because they would be competing against able-bodied handlers and their dogs, Rose and Kathleen needed to learn how to manage tight turns and pace changes from the wheelchair. With the help of a teacher assistant, Kathleen did daily upper-body exercises to strengthen her arms enough to handle the workload. They didn't want Rose to be penalized for not being able to change quickly enough from "normal" to "fast" pace. "For Rose," says Judi, "the hardest exercise was the 'figure eight,' and she learned to keep her eyes on that wheelchair, no matter what."

But dogs work best when they love their handler, and Rose belonged heart and soul to Judi. How could Kathleen win her over? Judi knew that Rose's performance depended entirely on Kathleen's ability as a handler, so she pushed Kathleen constantly to improve. Be firm. Be clear. Be consistent. Give the dog lots of praise. Finally, Kathleen got angry. "How come it's always me?" she demanded one day. "You never tell her what she should be doing!"

Judi Snowdon proudly displays one of Tuxedo Rose's many awards. SUSIE PITMAN

"Well, Kathleen," Judi responded, "Rose can only do what you direct her to do. She needs to have the commands and signals given the same way every time. She needs to have the wheelchair move the same speed and change direction exactly the same each time. She needs for you to be a bit more encouraging and a bit less demanding. When you call Rose, I want to see her run to you like she used to, not walk toward you like it's an effort."

Kathleen looked completely discouraged, but Judi wasn't finished. "You are going to be competing against people like me in that fun match, not against people like you. And that takes more work. You have the best dog, so treat her like she's the best dog and she'll work for you. You're doing okay, but you need to do better if you're going to compete. This isn't about marks. This is about life."

Suddenly, something changed in Kathleen. When she looked at Rose, she saw another creature who got discouraged sometimes. She realized that Rose needed to be appreciated and praised just as much as she did. "Sorry, Rose," she said. It was the breakthrough Judi had hoped for.

The training progressed to the point where Judi felt Kathleen and Rose were ready to participate in an actual competition, so she entered them in an upcoming event. Still, Judi couldn't help but worry; she knew that a dog's performance during obedience trials is always unpredictable. Kathleen said she would be okay with a low mark, but would she really?

On the morning of the Perfect Pooches obedience fun match, in spite of their progress, Kathleen was petrified. She sat waiting her turn, trembling and fidgeting, when suddenly the door opened and a man with a television camera came in and made his way toward her. He wanted to interview her for a special news segment. Not only was Kathleen going to compete, but she was also going to be on television! In spite of her nervousness, Kathleen rose to the occasion, answering the reporter's questions with unexpected poise.

But it was Kathleen and Rose's performance itself that truly amazed Judi. "Her 'figure eight' was wonderful," she says. "The 'stand for exam' was perfect; the 'sits' and 'downs' were perfect." The only thing Rose still balked at was the "finish"—returning to the heel position. Kathleen had to be very firm with Rose, insisting that she obey. "I stood there and thought 'please Rose, please let this happen!'" says Judi.

And Rose did. When the judging was complete and the total scores were added up, Kathleen and Rose were awarded a mark of 184 out of a possible 200 for their performance. Not only had they passed, they had passed with flying colours! Judi's own higher-scoring performance with Tuxedo Rose's sister, Smokey Rose, couldn't hold a candle to what Kathleen had just accomplished.

For Rose, that day was just one of a string of shining moments that would end all too soon. After a summer of prizewinning agility and sheep-herding competitions, Judi decided Rose needed a rest. They'd get back into their beloved dog sports next season, after a long, quiet winter. But Rose never had another summer. When Snowdon noticed Rose seemed to be feeling under the weather, she took her to visit the veterinarian. After much poking and prodding, the veterinarian ordered blood tests and X-rays, but Judi wasn't overly concerned. Rose was only seven years old and a strong, stoic dog. It never occurred to Judi that Rose could be sick.

But she was. On March 20, 2002, the first day of spring, Judi Snowdon and the students of Isabelle Sellon School lost their beloved Tuxedo Rose to leukemia. "I received over 200 messages of sympathy from the students, who truly shared my sorrow," recalls Judi. It was a harsh blow for Judi, but she's grateful that Rose was able to touch so many lives and so vividly illustrate the value of the human–animal bond.

For Kathleen, life continues to hold many challenges. But no matter what she faces, nothing can take away the gift she received from Rose that day in the ring: the gift of success.

CHAPTER

5

My Eyes Have Four Legs

THE WORK OF A SEEING EYE dog is often misunderstood. Guide dogs, according to celebrated children's author Jean Little, aren't heroes. Instead, they save their people from needing heroes. Legally blind from birth, Jean knows what she's talking about. "A good guide dog keeps you from getting into a dangerous situation," she says. "They don't pull you from beneath the wheels of a bus. They keep you from getting in front of the bus in the first place."

Jean's present guide dog, Pippa, is a quiet Labrador retriever who does her job without fanfare. During one recent visit to a friend's home, Jean noticed that every time she got up to move from one room to another, Pippa would get up, amble to a certain spot, then stand there and wait for

Jean to come back. Jean didn't think anything of it until she realized that there was an open staircase at that spot. Pippa was just making sure that Jean didn't tumble down a flight of stairs on her way to the bathroom.

Sighted people sometimes underestimate the importance of the concentration required for guide dogs to do their work. Jean's dogs wear the harness of working guide dogs, which identifies them, but she wishes people would explain more clearly to children what that means. "People say, 'Don't pet him, he's a working dog.' It doesn't make sense." Better, she argues, to say, "Don't *distract* him, he needs to concentrate."

Actually, both the dog and the handler need to concentrate. It takes careful observation of a dog's behaviour to catch all the cues, and Jean has had her share of mishaps. Rarely, though, have the dogs been to blame. Most of the time, Jean takes full responsibility herself. Several times when she's walked into something or fallen, she's been ready to snap out a reprimand, only to discover that the dog had already stopped. Had she been paying attention, she would have known she was supposed to stop also. On one occasion however, Jean was almost involved in a deadly traffic accident, and it wasn't due to an error on the part of either herself or her dog. Instead, it was because a sighted woman she knew had seen the pair and called to them. The dog looked up and missed the curb. As a result, Jean missed the curb as well and stumbled forward into the path of oncoming cars. Jean recalls how angry she was at her close call. "I can just see the headlines: Woman Led to Death by Guide Dog," she says. "Not what it should have been: Blind Person Dies Because Stupid Sighted Woman Distracted Guide Dog."

Although she was born with a visual disability, Jean didn't use a guide dog until relatively late in life. But then, she had always been extremely independent. Born in Taiwan in 1932 to missionary-doctor parents, Jean moved to Canada at the age of seven. Despite her disability, she attended regular classes in elementary and secondary school and went on to receive her BA in English language and literature from the University of Toronto. Books and stories had always been important in her life, and it was only natural for her to seek to share this love with young people. When she finished her studies, she took a teaching position at the Guelph Crippled Children's Centre in Guelph, Ontario.

Because she understood what it meant to be a handicapped child, Jean quickly developed a rapport with her students. She knew what it was like to be left out or overlooked, to feel different, angry and embarrassed. She remembered how it had helped her as a child to know the clinical terms for her condition, so she taught her students to face insensitive questions with straight answers. Soon the children in her classroom could reel off complicated medical terms such as "muscular dystrophy," "cerebral palsy" and "spastic quadriplegia." If you live with it, her motto seemed to be, you should also be able to name it.

Jean encouraged the children to read widely, often bringing in her own childhood favourites to read aloud. Characters with handicaps were of great interest, of course, but after teaching for several years, she realized that all the children's books dealing with disability focused on the characters overcoming their condition somehow. Usually, they were either cured or they died. "It's as if book publishers didn't think that a book could have a happy ending if the person was still in a wheelchair at the end," she says wryly.

So, Jean set out to change that. Her first novel, *Mine for Keeps*, is about the adventures of a child with cerebral palsy—who still has cerebral palsy at the end of the book. It was published in 1962 and won the Little, Brown Canadian Children's Book Award. "People think handicapped people are always sad," Jean says, "but I'm happier than most people I know who aren't handicapped."

Both teaching and writing are demanding occupations, and Jean soon admitted she couldn't do both. Writing won out, and she reluctantly left the classroom. She never, however, left children. Since *Mine for Keeps*, she has published 36 books for young readers. Her books have been translated into 10 different languages, and she has won eight literary awards. She's taught children's literature at the University of Guelph and is adjunct professor in the department of English. She's been the featured speaker at countless conferences, and she travels widely, talking about her dearest love: stories. Children line up for hours to get autographed copies of her books and ask questions. She is frequently asked why someone who clearly enjoys the company of children never married and had some of her own. To the delight of parents and teachers in the audience, she answers, straight-faced, "Some mistakes I've never made."

But while she never had children, Jean usually had a variety of animals in her life. Still, she couldn't have predicted how much her four-footed companions would one day mean to her.

By 1963, the birth defect that had scarred both her eyes had progressed to glaucoma. The pressure and swelling led to acutely painful corneal blisters, and as more time passed, it became apparent that her left eye had to be removed. She wasn't left totally blind; the vision in her right eye came and went, sometimes allowing her to distinguish shapes and patches of light and dark. However, every eye pain or migraine headache reminded her of the very real possibility of losing her right eye to glaucoma as well.

Then, an unexpectedly severe depression hit. Jean had always been able to cope with the limited vision she had, but the possibility of going totally blind terrified her. The only thing that might possibly be good about blindness, she admitted grudgingly, would be getting a guide dog. Friends and family suggested that she might be eligible for a Seeing Eye dog. Why didn't she apply and find out? Finally, in 1982, she filled out an application form. In April of that year, she received word that she'd been accepted to receive a dog and needed to be in Morristown, New Jersey, on August 15 for training. Her adventure with her first guide dog—Zephyr— was about to begin.

And what an adventure it was! Jean had never imagined that having a guide dog would make her life anything but easier. Why should she expect any problems? After all, she'd had dogs most of her life, and she'd been legally blind most of her life. She was good with dogs, and she was accustomed to her disability. But when Zephyr entered her life, he brought more than guidance. He brought challenge, fear and despair. He also brought inspiration; Jean's book *Stars Come Out Within* tells, among other things, the story of how she and Zephyr finally overcame their problems and learned to work together.

By the time he first met Jean, Zephyr, a naturally big-hearted dog, had already formed—and lost—two strong attachments in his young life. He'd been lovingly cared for by both the family who had raised him for the first year and the trainer who had prepared him for his new job. He was friendly with Jean, but reserved. She sensed it would take some time for him to risk further heartbreak.

Jean, however, had no such reservations. Awestruck by the intelligence this big dog exhibited, she had a hard time reprimanding him for anything. He already knew so much and obeyed so readily that nothing prepared her for the problems they'd face once they left the training centre.

Like all dogs, guide dogs for the blind need time and

training to become accustomed to their new life. But because guide dogs have already had so much specialized training, people often expect too much of them. Zephyr, a powerful yellow Labrador retriever, had the problem-solving abilities needed to be an exceptional guide dog. Unfortunately, he was also an alpha dog, waiting for the opportunity to assert himself and wrest control from his handler.

His opportunity came shortly after he and Jean left the training facility. Jean, thrilled with her new canine companion, couldn't wait to show off the independence he provided. When Zephyr first began to test her authority, she was so afraid of having to admit failure, so terrified that all her hopes of independence would be dashed, that she ignored the warning signs. These signs started slowly: an unhurried response here, an ignored command there. But soon, Zephyr had the bit between his teeth. Although he'd been raised and trained in the company of other dogs, now he found, in the more tolerant atmosphere of Jean's home, the opportunity to show off his superior power to every dog he met. His dominant personality rose to the surface, making him unwilling or unable to resist letting other dogs know who was boss.

At first, strange dogs merely distracted him. But as more time passed, he began to bark and growl at them. Eventually, he became obsessed with even a glimpse of other dogs, straining at the harness, leaping up and doing everything in his power to get at them. Jean began to dread going for walks. She avoided streets where she knew dogs lived. She tried everything she could think of to correct his behaviour, but nothing had any effect. In every other way, however, he was a perfect guide dog. "I almost gave up on Zephyr," recalls Jean, who at 50 was older than most first-time guide-dog recipients. "When you get a dog and have problems it's a great shock." However, Jean had grown to love Zephyr and couldn't bear the thought of losing him. She knew they couldn't go on as they were, but she couldn't give up on him either.

Then came the winter day when Zephyr saw a poodle inside a passing car. He went berserk, dragging Jean into five lanes of traffic, barely missing cars, deaf to screeching tires, blaring horns and the screams of his owner.

When she finally made it home that day, shaken and fighting back tears, she went straight to the phone and called the centre where she and Zephyr had trained. Seeing Eye, Inc., in Morristown, New Jersey, is the oldest guide-dog school in North America. The behavioural problems Jean described to them sounded so severe that they immediately offered her a new dog. Jean begged for another option. Couldn't someone come down and help them? In a last-ditch effort, trainer Dan Boeke stepped in to work with the pair. Jean told him about Zephyr's tendencies, and then the three of them went for a walk. Zephyr wasted no time disgracing himself, and Boeke was appalled. Grimly, he warned Jean not to get her hopes up, then he took hold of the harness himself. He knew that their only chance lay in drastic measures—and he was merciless. Zephyr had met his match.

Within a day, everything changed. "Zephyr just needed somebody strong who knew what to do," Jean says. The strategy was simple: Zephyr had to be shown, in no uncertain terms, that he was not the boss. Jean was horrified to see her big dog jerked off his feet, slammed to the ground, yanked into position and hollered at like a cadet at boot camp. The slightest growl earned him a terrific punishment, both verbal and physical, and the more he resisted, the more Boeke piled it on. Finally, Zephyr admitted defeat. Jean began to believe there might be hope after all.

But only, Boeke emphasized, if she used the same techniques herself. Jean steeled herself to dominate Zephyr and ignore his beseeching appeals for leniency. It had to be done, and it was hard, but it worked. Zephyr reluctantly deferred to Jean's authority. The next step was rewarding him for good behaviour. For Zephyr, this meant one thing: food. They practised incessantly, walking up and down every dog-filled street Jean could find. Whenever she heard another dog bark, she knew Zephyr was working hard to control himself. Praising him extravagantly, she'd give him a treat. Zephyr had been reminded of his job and was willing, once again, to do it wholeheartedly. "It got to where he was making faces at the other dogs, trying to get them to bark so I'd give him a treat," she laughs.

It was the turning point in their relationship. Jean,

already well published by then, did what she always did with the significant events in her life. She wrote about them, with typical honesty. "No one was talking about the problems," she says. "I decided it was time someone wrote about the first year with a dog, from the perspective of the blind person." *Stars Come Out Within* continues the autobiographical tale begun in *Little by Little*, which tells the story of her adolescent years as a blind child.

After Jean and Zephyr's rough start, an amazing tale of teamwork began. Jean had learned to be firm with Zephyr, and soon she would learn to trust him. One afternoon, during a sweltering Ontario summer, Jean made the mistake of going shopping downtown with Zephyr. "We were outside, just walking along, and the heat was burning my feet," she recalls. "I figured it must be torture for Zephyr's feet." She decided to turn around and head for home. But Zephyr had a better idea. Although he was familiar with the route they'd taken, he suddenly took a different turn. "He had no reason to turn," says Jean. "I should have corrected him, but I was curious."

She let him walk, wondering what he had in mind. He kept on going, purposefully walking across the sidewalk and up a set of steps until Jean realized they were inside a city bus. He flopped down and turned toward her, waiting patiently for her to catch on. "He looked at me as if to say, 'Lady if you want to walk, walk. I'm taking the bus.'" But you can't just get on any bus—it has to be the right one.

Jean imagined herself and the dog lost, travelling back and forth across the city for the rest of the day. She approached the driver apologetically, asking which bus she was on and where it was headed. "Turns out it went right past my corner! So, we just sat down and took the bus home." From then on, Jean enjoyed telling everyone that because her dog had chosen the right bus out of a lineup, he must be able to read. But, she adds, when she got home and tried to get him to read something else to her, he wasn't interested. "He told me it wasn't in his job description," she jokes.

The job of learning to trust Zephyr was more difficult than Jean expected, and sometimes it was hard to know whether or not he really knew what he was doing. One time when the pair was walking to the library, Zephyr refused to take Jean across the street at the usual corner. At that particular corner, five streets came together, making a wheel-like intersection. "I said to Zephyr, forward!" says Jean. "He stood there and looked to where I was pointing. Then he turned and went the other way—four crossings over—until he got to the same spot." Jean bit back her annoyance. The trainers, after all, had reminded them constantly to put their faith in the dogs, so she repeated to herself what they told her: "Your dog can see. You cannot." When they finally got across the street, a woman stopped her to comment on how smart Zephyr was. "Smart dog? Smart?" Jean responded indignantly. "He should have crossed way back there!" Then the woman explained what Zephyr already knew: a road-construction crew was working on the sewer right where they usually crossed, making the path too narrow for both to cross safely. "He'd have fit through but I'd have been hit," Jean says. "He wouldn't go because of me."

Zephyr lived with Jean for 10 years, at which time guide dogs are usually retired. By then, the duo had naturally become extremely close, but Jean needed a dog young and strong enough to do the job. Many retired guide dogs live out their senior years with their owners, but Jean lived alone at that time and felt she couldn't handle two dogs by herself. She found Zephyr a home with a family who wanted a big dog for their children and who would still let her visit him. She feared he'd pine for her and was rather taken aback to discover that, while he was always thrilled to see her, the sociable dog enjoyed life with his new family.

Since Zephyr, Jean rarely travels without a dog at her side. After him came Ritz, and then Pippa, and each guide dog has found a special spot in Jean's heart. But the challenges she faced with Zephyr created something unique. "He was my first, so there was a deeper bond," she says. "You spend more time with a guide dog than you do with any human being."

Jean, who has been the recipient of numerous prestigious awards, including the Order of Canada, doesn't take herself too seriously. Perhaps attending awards ceremonies with her dogs helps keep her grounded. "You should see these guide dogs walking in honorary procession," she laughs. "They certainly behave themselves. But then they'll start chewing their foot in the middle of it, or licking themselves."

Perhaps more than anything else, Jean values the way her dogs have helped her make connections with those around her. Many people, she's found, are afraid to initiate a conversation with a blind person. In her pre-dog days when she'd attend one of her frequent conferences or speaking engagements, she often felt lonely. "I didn't know where anyone was or if anyone was looking at me," she remembers. But now that a guide dog always accompanies her, people readily approach her to comment on how beautiful her dog is.

A dog, she says, acts as a wonderful bridge between her and the sighted world. "Now, if no one's talking to me, I talk to my dog. It makes me look engaged, rather than pitiable." If anything, she adds, she feels enviable. "A lot of people would love to have one of these dogs."

6

Not My Dog

ONE OF THE MOST SATISFYING aspects of working in the field of veterinary medicine is the occasional opportunity to play matchmaker. When animals are relinquished into our care that we cannot bear to euthanize, we adopt them ourselves or find homes for them with friends and relatives. When our friends and relatives stop taking our calls, we know we have a problem.

Every now and then, though, it's not a pet that needs a home as much as it is a person who needs a pet. This situation took place many years ago, and I've employed creative licence with certain details; however, I've never forgotten the heart of the story.

The thump of metal against glass was, as usual, the first

thing to announce that Cecil Price had arrived. Dr. Richards looked up from his desk, where he was writing files, wondering what was wrong with little Benji today, if anything. Mr. Price propped the end of his cane against the door, while he negotiated the dog, the leash and his prosthetic leg through the doorway. The old man had a regular walking routine that probably took hours. Rain or shine, he appeared on the sidewalks around town every day, his faithful Benji always at his side. He often showed up at our clinic without an appointment, just to weigh his dog or chat about the weather. We'd long suspected that Mr. Price's visits were more social than medical.

I showed Mr. Price and Benji into a room and chatted with him while Dr. Richards donned his stethoscope and lab coat. "Mr. Price, how are you?" The vet gently shook the frail hand extended toward him.

"Cecil, Doc, Cecil. How many times do I have to tell you? You're too young to have memory problems. Maybe once you get to my age," he answered with a laugh.

I lifted Benji onto the table for his examination. The dog had numerous health problems, mostly due to bad breeding and neglect suffered before he came to live with Mr. Price. Benji was Maltese crossed with poodle and possibly something else, but his ancestry and puppyhood were a mystery. Mr. Price's son had adopted him for his father from a shelter a few years previous, hoping to ease the old man's loneliness after the death of his wife. It was a brilliant move. Mr. Price had seen through the obesity, the horrible skin and bad breath and recognized the sweet, gentle creature beneath. Immediately, he'd brought him to Dr. Richards for, in his words, "an overhaul," after which he'd launched an exercise program to return Benji to fitness.

Mr. Price's son had given his father an enormous gift; caring for Benji had pulled the elderly widower out of his grief and depression and given him a reason to get up in the morning.

"He's scratching again," said Mr. Price, pointing a trembling, gnarled finger at a spot behind Benji's ear. "And he's been bringing up his food. Sometimes he won't eat his dinner at all."

Dr. Richards looked at the hot spot. Benji's allergies were acting up again, as pollens and parasites began their usual springtime reign of terror. He'd never be able to cure Benji's reactive skin, but he could at least treat the discomfort.

The vomiting was a different issue. As was the lack of appetite. As was the ominous mass we found in the dog's belly. A week later, test results confirmed that Benji had a malignant tumour.

"He's an old dog," said Mr. Price. "I don't want him to suffer."

"We can keep him comfortable for a few more weeks," Dr. Richards said, hating that it was all he had to offer. "It will give you time to prepare yourself. Spend time doing his favourite things. You'll know when it's time."

For six weeks, Mr. Price continued as usual. At first, it was walks as usual. He popped in every few days so we could have a look at Benji. Day by day, the little dog shrank before our eyes. But he still wagged his tail and licked our hands and watched his master with adoration in his black eyes.

"Not time yet," said Mr. Price, and we agreed.

Then he changed his route, shortening it by a few blocks. It took longer, despite the shorter distance. One day, the door opened with an even louder crash and bang. Mr. Price arrived with a battered stroller in front of him. Benji was sitting in the stroller, panting, looking around him with interest.

"He gets too tired, but he still wants to see all his friends," explained Mr. Price. "And I let him out to sniff his favourite spots."

The dog's ribs were now easily felt beneath the silky fur, and he only took a polite sniff of the liver treat Dr. Richards offered him. But his eyes still sparkled and his tail wagged.

"Not time yet," said Mr. Price. Dr. Richards nodded. Soon, but not yet.

Then Mr. Price showed up leaning on his cane again, with Benji tucked inside a baby sling. The little dog licked at my finger and wagged his tail, but when I picked him up, he felt insubstantial as air. When Dr. Richards began his examination, Benji was too weak to stand.

"I think . . . ," said Mr. Price with a trembling voice, "is it . . . ? What do you think, Doc?"

It was time. Mr. Price was a brave man, staying through-out the procedure to comfort his little friend to the end. But as the old man limped out of the office, his sling hanging empty over his shoulder, we worried about how this loss would hit him.

It was several weeks before we realized we hadn't seen Mr. Price on his usual walks. Dr. Richards telephoned his house. No answer. Our concern grew until one day Dr. Richards thought to contact his son. Mr. Price, he learned, wasn't well. He hadn't left the house in days. He barely left his chair. He wasn't eating. "He's so lonely," the son reported. "I don't know what to do. He misses Mom. His friends are all dead. Now Benji's gone too. I think he's just waiting to die. Any chance you could pop by to say hello?"

Dr. Richards decided a house call was in order, and when he returned, he looked shaken. The old man appeared to have aged a decade overnight, he told us. His clothes hung on him, and he hadn't changed them in days. But he walked as well as before, and his mind was as sharp as ever.

"I told him he should get another dog," said Dr. Richards, shaking his head. "But he says he's too old. He's going to die soon and then what would happen to it?"

It seemed a hopeless situation, and although Dr. Richards tried to respect their professional relationship and the bound-aries that came with that, we could tell it weighed on him. Then one day the SPCA dropped by with an abandoned dog they wanted him to examine. The little creature was a mess. Dr. Richards estimated his age at between five and eight. He was an intact male, overweight, with horrible teeth, bald patches on his belly and large clumps of matted fur behind his ears. But he was affectionate and quiet, and somewhere along the way, he'd learned "sit" and "down."

"Leave him with me," Dr. Richards said with a smile. As soon as the shelter constable left, we descended on our project dog, whom we called Benji Two.

I refused to let him into our operating room without a bath and a haircut, so that was first. Then we neutered him, removed a couple of warts, extracted three rotten teeth, cleaned the remaining ones and finally cleaned all the hair, dirt and wax out of his ears. By the end of the day, Benji Two was a different dog.

We gave him a few days to recover and to assure ourselves that he had no other health or behaviour issues. In that time, we fell in love with him. He'd be perfect for Mr. Price. Now for the tricky part: convincing Mr. Price.

Dr. Richards picked up the telephone. It was a short conversation, and it didn't go as we'd hoped. "He says it wouldn't be fair," Dr. Richards said, his shoulders sagging with disappointment. "He won't even consider it. I can't think of anyone else who might want him. None of us can take another dog, and our zoning won't let us keep him here permanently. No, Mr. Price was his only hope."

He walked back to the treatment room where Benji Two

was resting in a cage. I followed, the glimmer of an idea in my mind.

"He could still find a home at the shelter." Dr. Richards sounded as if he was trying to convince himself.

I shook my head. "In puppy season? Not likely. You said it right from the beginning, Boss, he's Mr. Price's dog." I paused. "We just won't tell Mr. Price that."

Dr. Richards looked at me in confusion for a moment, then, as I handed him a leash, understanding dawned. "Come on, little guy," he said, slipping the collar over the scruffy neck. "Let's go for a walk. I want you to meet someone."

It was a lovely day for a walk. Benji Two waddled behind us, pausing now and then to sniff the shrubbery. He politely greeted the other people and dogs we passed by. Dr. Richards stepped up to Mr. Price's front door and knocked. After a long pause, we heard a shuffling sound and the deadbolt clicked open. Cecil Price was in worse shape than before. His skin was sallow, his eyes sunken. He was disappearing, bit by bit.

"I'd like you to meet our new mascot," said Dr. Richards. "He was going to be put down, and since you couldn't take him, I figured we could keep him at the clinic. I call him Benji Two, because he looks so much like your Benji."

Mr. Price extended a trembling hand to the ugly little dog. "He's the spitting image, isn't he, Doc? I'm glad you saved him."

We visited for a few minutes and then left with Benji Two. As we turned the corner, I looked over my shoulder and saw Mr. Price watching us from the doorway.

Two days later, Mr. Price appeared on the street with his cane again, more stooped than he'd been before, but walking nevertheless. He thumped and banged through the clinic door, smiling tentatively.

"I needed to get some exercise again," he said, looking around the waiting room. "I thought I'd come in and say hello to Benji Two."

"Cecil!" said Dr. Richards, bringing the dog with him from the back room. "I thought I heard you come in. Look who's here, boy. Go say hello."

Benji Two trotted up to Mr. Price and sat down, his tongue lolling through a gap of missing teeth. Mr. Price bent down awkwardly and ran a gnarled hand over the dog's head.

"Hey, maybe you could help me out," said Dr. Richards, as if the idea had just occurred to him. "We're all going out of town for a conference this weekend. I need someone to look after Benji Two. Would you mind?"

Mr. Price didn't hesitate. He took Benji Two with him that afternoon, with the agreement that the dog would return to the clinic on Monday morning. And on Monday morning, bright and early, he was back.

"How'd everything go?" I asked.

"Great," said Mr. Price, smiling at Benji Two. He stood a

little straighter, and the colour had returned to his cheeks. "It was just like having my old Benji back."

"He looks like he enjoyed himself." I wondered if I should push a little harder. But before I could, Mr. Price handed the leash over.

"It's like what they say about grandchildren," he said. "You enjoy them more because you know they're leaving soon and someone else is in charge of the real work."

As he turned to go, however, Benji Two whined and pulled at the leash to follow him. I dropped the leash, and the little dog ran to Mr. Price and jumped up against his legs.

"Benji," scolded Mr. Price. "We talked about this."

"Cecil," began Dr. Richards, and I knew he was going for the hard sell. But Mr. Price didn't let him get that far.

"I told you, Doc," he interrupted. "I can't have another dog. You need to understand. I've only got a few years left. Probably less. Benji Two belongs to you."

Then he dipped his head and smiled at the dog. "But I suppose, if you insist, I could help you out now and then."

I understood. Mr. Price could only commit himself so far. He wasn't afraid of dying for his own sake, but he couldn't bear to take another dog only to inadvertently abandon him. It took a moment longer for Dr. Richards to hear what Mr. Price couldn't say, but finally it clicked into place.

"As long as you know he's not your dog," said Dr. Richards, reeling Benji Two in. "We couldn't give him up now. He's

our mascot. He's got his own fan club already. I just thought
that if you're out walking anyway . . ."

"He can walk with me." Mr. Price smiled.

"It would really help us out." Dr. Richards bent down
and scratched the little dog behind the ear. "He gets pretty
bored here on busy days."

"He's good company, aren't you, boy?" Mr. Price straight-
ened himself up as much as he could.

"As long as you don't forget," said Dr. Richards sternly,
"that he's not your dog."

"He's not my dog." Mr. Price's voice was hoarse as he
looked down at Benji Two. He cleared his throat and swallowed hard. When he lifted his head, his eyes sparkled with
unshed tears. "Thanks, Doc."

CHAPTER

7

In the Water

IF YOU DON'T WANT TO BE dragged back to shore, say Newfoundland dog enthusiasts, don't go swimming with a Newf. As far as these big dogs are concerned, people belong on dry land. If they think someone is in danger of drowning, they'll do everything in their power to come to the rescue.

When a warm body hits cold water, muscles contract with shock, making it impossible to draw breath. Even strong swimmers can be virtually paralyzed within moments, certain to drown without aid. And, unless dressed in protective gear, would-be rescuers are at risk of suffering the same fate. But for the huge, sea-loving Newfoundlands, with their naturally water-repellent fur and tremendous lung capacity, making a rescue in frigid water is a piece of cake.

In the Water

Denise Castonguay of CastaNewf Kennels in Maple Ridge, British Columbia, saw vivid proof of this skill several years ago during a lakeside training session with Mister, a young Newfoundland male bred at her kennel and sold to close family friends. Castonguay works on her dogs' water-rescue skills each year at beautiful Buntzen Lake, between Coquitlam and Port Moody. A popular tourist destination, the lake is clear, clean and stocked with fish. It's also one of the few lakes that allows dogs and has a boat launch, two essentials for water training.

Although all the dogs are worked in each session, Castonguay focuses on achieving a title with one specific dog every summer. This is no small task. Newfoundlands who have reached Junior Water Dog status have already learned to perform a number of small tasks on command: retrieving a life jacket from the water; taking a rope to a stranger who is pretending to drown; and towing to shore a stranded boat, four to five metres long, made of heavy aluminum. Senior Water Dog titleholders have learned to do the more difficult tasks of distinguishing between several items to be retrieved or people needing to be rescued. They also must take a rope out to a stranded boat and tow it ashore, and they must find and retrieve an item dropped to the lake floor. These underwater retrieves are tricky because some dogs resist getting their heads wet.

But the most difficult task to teach is what's called a "swim with handler." In this task, dog and trainer swim side by side within an arm's length of each other. After swimming about six metres, the handler goes into a limp free-float. The handler then grabs on to the dog, who must tow his "victim" back to shore. Usually, the dogs happily perform the return trip but really resist the swim out. "It's one of the hardest things to train, because a really instinctual dog will do anything he can to keep you out of the water," says Castonguay, "including body blocking you or herding you back to shore."

Castonguay will never forget one particular day at Buntzen Lake. It was a hot, cloudless morning, and she knew the sun worshippers would be out in force. Castonguay and her group of dogs and trainers arrived early in an attempt to avoid the crowds, but by the time they'd finished their work the park was already filled to capacity.

They had just finished loading their boat back onto the trailer when a group of teenagers arrived on the dock. The dogs watched them, whining and pulling at their leads. Because they would never come out of the water voluntarily, the dogs were all tied to trees until their handlers were free to put them into the vehicles. As the dogs waited, each teenaged whoop and holler and every splash off the dock wound them up a little more until they were all pining to get back into the lake. "The dogs were very focused on this group who were jumping and diving off the end of the dock," says Castonguay. "They were a rowdy bunch, racing each other back and forth from the dock area to a rocky outpoint a few hundred yards away." Castonguay and the other handlers tried to ignore the barking and whining. The dogs were only following their instinctive drive; they had no way of knowing the commotion was nothing more than kids having fun. Still, it was quite a racket, and Castonguay and her friends hurried to pack up and get away before the dogs became more upset.

Mister, in particular, could barely contain himself. Although he's now the most successful of her dogs, currently holding 17 titles for his various skills, at that time he was just getting started. The temptation was more than his youthful enthusiasm and energy could withstand. Finally, in a frenzy, he broke free and flew straight for the end of the dock, full speed, all 100-plus pounds of him. By that time, the rest of the dogs had caught his excitement, and as he plunged into the water, they increased their chorus of frantic barking.

Castonguay tried everything she could think of to get Mister back to shore, but he ignored her. "He was not coming," she says. "He was circling at the end of the dock, whining. We couldn't entice him with anything, not toys, not cookies, nothing."

The teenagers had formed a circle at the end of the dock, yelling and screaming, and Castonguay knew she needed to get Mister out of there as soon as possible. The only thing left to do was head back into the water and drag him out. "We had to unload the boat from the trailer, row out and physically grab him by the collar," she says.

There were by then so many people at the dock that

Castonguay suspected something else must have happened. Even after being unceremoniously hauled out of the water, Mister remained intent on the crowd near the dock, so as soon as they reached the shore, Castonguay locked him securely inside her vehicle. "By the time we got the boat secured again," recalls Castonguay, "an ambulance had arrived." Much later in the day, they learned the full story of what had happened, the incident Mister and the other dogs had sensed. One of the boys had dived off the end of the dock and hadn't come up. "They had to call in divers to retrieve his body," she says.

Castonguay was astonished to learn that Mister had been circling the water over exactly the same place where the body was later recovered. "Mister knew where to go but not what to do once he got there," she says. "An older, more experienced dog might have attempted to dive."

Castonguay, who currently has 14 Newfoundlands of varying ages, has almost 20 years of experience in breeding and training, and in achieving championships in the conformation ring. In addition to water work, she also trains her dogs in obedience and draft work, aiming to preserve the purpose for which her dogs were originally bred. "We strive to do it all with our Newfs," she says. But still, Mister's exhibit of natural talent left her awestruck. "I've seen them do some pretty basic things that other people think are amazing, but this to me was a real indication of their life-saving ability," she says. "Pure instinct told him to disregard his restraint and ignore our commands."

An Italian drypoint by Amos Nattini illustrating the Newfoundland as ship dog. AMOS NATTINI

For well over 200 years, the Newfoundland breed has been invaluable to fishermen and sailors who work in and around the frigid waters of the northeastern Canadian coast. Various theories exist to explain the appearance of these big, black dogs on their native island of Newfoundland. Dog experts speculate that their ancestry includes everything from early European explorers' dogs to mastiffs, sheepdogs and wolves. In their famous expedition to the Pacific Northwest of the United States, Lewis and Clark had a dog with them named Scannon, who is thought to have been a Newfoundland. By the 18th century, the breed had gained some uniformity in appearance and had begun to increase in both numbers and popularity, but it was during the 19th century that breeders developed the characteristics we recognize in today's Newfoundland dog.

No matter what the origins of the breed, their early purpose was clear: to assist fishermen in their work in and around the water. The dogs were used for a variety of tasks. They helped to haul in heavy, wet nets loaded with fish and spent a fair amount of time retrieving items such as ropes from the water. But often they did much more. One famous Newf named Tang received the Lloyd's Medal for Meritorious Service in 1919 after performing a dramatic rescue off the coast of Nova Scotia. Tang was aboard a ship that was being dashed against the rocky shoreline by a vicious December storm. The last hope of survival for the 92 people on board was for someone to carry a line to shore. One sailor attempted it but was quickly lost in the gale. Tang saw this and stepped up to grab the line. When his captain gave the command, Tang leapt into the ocean and managed to bring the line to a group of people on shore, who were then able to complete the rescue. Everyone on board was saved.

On the open ocean, making rope connection to land can mean the difference between life and death. But sometimes it's simply a matter of convenience. At Buntzen Lake, Castonguay has often seen vacationers in their rental canoes, paddling in circles and sitting on their lifejackets with no idea what they're doing. Usually they make it back to the dock, awkwardly but in one piece. But one day she saw two young girls stranded motionless in their canoe, about 45 metres from shore. They'd lost their paddles, and to make things worse, they spoke almost no English. Castonguay was preparing a dog named Sunny for her Senior Water Dog certification that year and thought it was a perfect opportunity for the dog to get some real-life practice. "We were yelling at them, trying to explain that we'd send a dog out with a line to tow them in," laughs Castonguay. But the girls didn't understand and were terrified of the dog. A hiker happened by just then who was able to translate, and he also tried to explain. "He shouted at them and they nodded, so we sent the dog out."

Sunny took the line and began swimming toward the boat. But when she got within range, the girls refused to take the line. They couldn't bring themselves to get close enough to the big dog. Sunny turned around to start towing them back, but stopped when she didn't feel the weight of the boat. She then swam back to the canoe to offer the rope again. Puzzled but determined, Sunny circled the boat several times until finally, when her back was turned, the girls gathered their courage and snatched the end of the rope. "The boat was a little different and the people were a little different," says Castonguay, "but other than that, it was exactly like what we do in our training exercises." Even with uncooperative "victims," Sunny knew what to do, and she did it. Who knows, she may have given them a story they'll tell for the rest of their lives.

Trigger Happy

MARSHA ARMSTRONG HAD HEARD OF Seeing-Eye dogs, but she never supposed dogs could help people with other disabilities. Indeed, she had no reason to even consider the notion—she had been healthy all her life. But in 1993, Marsha sat in her doctor's office in Burlington, Ontario, struggling to make sense of the words she was hearing. She'd just been diagnosed with an acoustic neuroma, an egg yolk–sized brain tumour that occurs in about one out of 500,000 people. The growth sat nestled on the eighth cranial nerve leading from the brain to the inner ear, an area affecting the muscles of the face as well as those that control balance. A tumour in this delicate area can have devastating results.

Several years earlier, Marsha, who works in the construction industry, had noticed that she was losing some of her hearing ability in one ear. She wasn't surprised; it's a common occupational hazard. What she didn't realize was that single-sided hearing loss, accompanied by ringing or buzzing—called tinnitus—is also the first symptom of this rare brain tumour. And the symptoms don't stop there.

Intermittent episodes of facial nerve paralysis, also called Bell's palsy, made Marsha suspect something more serious. "They figure I had the tumour for 10 years," Marsha says. It was a good news, bad news situation; acoustic neuromas are usually benign, but slowly and surely grow deeper into the brain stem, which is "command central" for the entire body. Marsha's surgeon told her that without surgery, she'd be dead within the year. However, he also warned her that surgery in this part of the brain was risky, and there was no guarantee that, even in the best-case scenario, her symptoms would disappear. When Marsha signed the consent form the day of the surgery, she knew it was a delicate procedure with potential for problems. She had no idea what sort of world she'd wake up to.

The procedure seemed to go well, and her tumour was successfully removed. She would live. But the surgeon's warnings proved prophetic. Marsha was left completely deaf in her left ear, and partially blind in her left eye. As another after-effect of the surgery, she also developed a condition called Ménière's disease. Its most frightening symptom is

84

severe vertigo, a balance disorder common in people with acoustic neuromas.

Balance problems, partial deafness and partial blindness may not seem debilitating; many people suffer worse disabilities, after all. But these conditions had profound effects on Marsha, partly, she thinks, because her handicaps aren't obvious. "I look perfectly fine," she says. "But I'll be walking down the hallway and suddenly drop to the floor." The simplest things suddenly became difficult. "The elevator, for instance," she says. "I have to think the whole way up and when I'm getting off." No longer could she drive her car or go dancing on Friday nights. Even a quiet walk outside was fraught with difficulty. On a couple of occasions, she misjudged the direction of sound and inadvertently moved right into the path of joggers approaching from behind— both times she was flattened as a result. Crawling into bed exhausted, she often found she couldn't relax enough to sleep. "It's scary to lie down at night and not be able to hear anything," she admits.

Under stress, her symptoms worsened, affecting her speech and causing one eyelid to droop. That's when people would notice something was wrong, but they still wouldn't necessarily suspect a disability. Instead, they'd treat her as if she was drunk, absent-minded or just plain thoughtless. "When people approach me from my left side or behind me, I don't hear or see them," she says. "People would speak to me in grocery stores, for example, perhaps wanting to get past me, and when I didn't respond I'd be bumped with carts or called rude names."

For several years, Marsha tried to adjust to her new life, but her once outgoing, extroverted personality began to fade under the weight of misunderstanding and prejudice. Even casual conversations were so difficult they seemed hardly worth the effort. "I lost my confidence and stopped going out in public," she remembers.

Then, one weekend in 1997, she had an experience that changed the rest of her life. She saw a group of people and dogs doing a demonstration for National Service Dogs (NSD). Marsha was surprised to learn that NSD trained hearing-ear dogs. Eagerly, she grabbed all the brochures and information pamphlets she could find and immediately contacted the organization to request a spot on its waiting list.

A long and anxious waiting period began. It takes a full year of training—at a cost of about $8,000 to $10,000—to teach an assistance dog all the specific tasks he'll be required to perform. NSD tries to find the best dog to fit each owner, and sometimes it takes additional time to make an appropriate match. Larger dogs such as Labrador retrievers, golden retrievers and German shepherds are well known for their abilities as assistance dogs. But Marsha worried about having such a large dog. "You're only too happy to get a dog at all," she says, "but I hoped it would work with my small home and my two cats."

Then the people at NSD introduced her to Trigger, a handsome Jack Russell terrier. Although he was large for his breed, he was much smaller than the Labrador retriever Marsha had been expecting. She was overjoyed! They were only allowed a brief period of time to get acquainted before Trigger was taken back to be trained in the specific tasks Marsha needed help with.

Marsha would soon discover there was a lot of dog packed into the compact breed NSD had chosen for her. The word "terrier" has its roots in the Latin *terre*, which means "earth." Like most terriers, Jack Russells were originally bred to "go to ground," hunting small rodents such as rats and mice. But these alert, feisty dogs have many other capabilities. They excel in sports such as flyball and agility and are popular companions for children. One Jack Russell terrier named Rats even attained international celebrity in the 1970s after "joining" a Northern Ireland army unit and surviving numerous bombings and sniper attacks. Today, these terriers are becoming more common as assistance and alert dogs, especially when a smaller dog is needed.

After three long months, Marsha and Trigger met again, this time to begin their training together. Professional trainers lay the foundation of general knowledge for each dog, but once a match is made, the dog has to learn the specific tasks required by his new owner. For six weeks, five days each week, Marsha and Trigger took intensive instruction from trainers on how to work together as a team. Trigger had to learn that Marsha, and only Marsha, was boss. Wherever Marsha went—even if it was to the bathroom—Trigger went too. "Trigger was attached to me all the time, even sleeping, by a long lead around my waist," she says. "He came to work with me for two weeks as well." It was hard, time-consuming work, but ultimately it cemented the bond necessary to form a successful working relationship. Marsha, however, is quick to credit their success to NSD trainers Heather Fowler and Danielle Forbes, whose patience and dedication have enriched the lives of so many people affected by disabilities.

What are Trigger's daily tasks? He is trained to alert Marsha to any important sounds that she might not hear herself. He informs her when the telephone, doorbell, alarm clock or stove timer rings. He's also trained to indicate the sound of the smoke detector, and he even taught himself to let her know when the buzzer on the clothes dryer goes off. Sometimes he'll even let Marsha know when trucks are beeping to back up. His method is simple, with a few variations. When the phone rings, Trigger runs to Marsha and jumps against her to let her know something's happening. Then he runs back, jumps onto the chair beside the phone and puts both paws on it. To alert her to the smoke detector, he jumps up against her to get her attention, then spins in circles. When the doorbell rings, he comes to her, then goes to the door and jumps up against it. And when the alarm clock rings in the morning, he jumps onto the bed and starts tugging at the blankets.

Trigger's companionship and dedication to his job has given Marsha Armstrong her life back. ANDRE CYR

He's also trained to recognize her name. When Trigger is out with Marsha's grandson Taylor, for instance, the boy can say "Marsha, Marsha! Get Marsha!" and Trigger will take him to wherever Marsha is. He's also learned Taylor's name, so Marsha can always find her grandson.

Although Trigger is not specifically trained to assist Marsha with her balance problems, he's taught himself to do what she needs. "He stays on my weaker side, as a buffer to keep me from bumping into people," she says. When fatigue causes her pace or step to change, Trigger adjusts his positioning. He makes sure he's slightly in front of her so she won't trip over him.

He's smart and strong, but he's still terrier to the core, which means he's also very stubborn. When guests are in the house, Trigger likes to lie down on the job, secure in the knowledge that others are there to help Marsha and alert her to various sounds. Even though she could let him off the hook, Marsha knows she has to be firm with him, and he grudgingly complies.

But one day in the grocery store, Marsha couldn't reprimand him. She had left Trigger in the truck, with the sliding window cracked for ventilation. He waited until she was out of sight, then nosed the window open, jumped out and found his way to the dairy section at the back of the store. Marsha reached for a jug of milk, looked down and there he was, casually trotting along behind her. She had thought she could do this one little job on her own, but the assistance dog who had changed her life thought differently. He had no intention of being left alone in the truck while she went shopping, not if he could avoid it. Helping her was his job, and nothing would stand in his way. "He just took his place without any fanfare," she says. "I didn't leave him very often, and he was familiar with the store. He thought he should be there with me."

Marsha has come a long way from those dark days after surgery. Between medication, therapy and Trigger's help, her physical abilities have improved dramatically, and she is once again able to tackle life with confidence. "He has a marvellous personality and he entertains me daily," she laughs. She's even able to drive during the day now. Trigger rides shotgun, ready and waiting for his next task. If she leaves him in the car, he waits for her to return, eyes straight ahead, even ignoring people who try to talk to him. "Then when I come back he turns around and barks at them like mad!" she laughs.

Marsha's emotional healing has been just as significant as her physical healing. Where her life once seemed to be an uphill battle full of bad days that kept getting worse, Trigger has brought a sense of competence, good fortune and even joy. "I'm not afraid to go out at night anymore," she says. "I am happy and healthy and outgoing again."

Marsha hit the jackpot with her little dog, and she knows it. Each day she is more grateful for Trigger's enthusiastic help and companionship. She's also become something of a crusader, educating people on the symptoms of acoustic neuroma and Ménière's disease. She hopes no one else will have to go through the lonely years of confusion and despair that she did. She also encourages people with less common disabilities to consider the benefits that an assistance dog could bring to their lives.

"It's hard to reflect on the sadness I felt at that time," she says. "I think I have done much better than a lot of people without dogs. I can't imagine not having a service dog."

CHAPTER

9

Terror in Moose Country

LEEANN O'REILLY WALKED THROUGH the quiet forest, keeping step to the rhythmic clang of the cowbell attached to her backpack. Her dogs, Rottweilers named Dakota and Max, ranged slightly ahead of her, circling back periodically. It was a chilly, late October afternoon in 1999, and they were just about ready to head back home when LeeAnn heard a crashing noise on the trail above her. She figured a falling tree branch had caused the noise, but then she saw that her dogs had stiffened. Watching them growl, their hackles raised, LeeAnn realized the noise must have been something else—something dangerous. A moment later, the blood froze in her veins as she came face to face with one of the most frightening eventualities of wilderness hiking: an angry moose charging straight toward her.

LeeAnn knows all about wilderness hazards. Moose, bear, caribou, bottomless bogs, disorienting forest and unpredictable weather—they're all considered part of the beauty of life on the "Rock" by this long-time resident of Corner Brook, Newfoundland. As an experienced outdoor adventurer and dog-sport enthusiast, LeeAnn loves having access to new areas to take her dogs hiking and tracking. Although she was born in Ontario, she can't imagine living anywhere else. "I stay here because of the environment," she says. "It's ideal for dogs."

And dogs are her life. LeeAnn works nights as a psychiatric nurse so that she's home during the day to run her private dog charity, By the Bay Rescue. In the past six years, she estimates that she and her volunteers have rescued over 500 homeless, unwanted or abused dogs. She tries not to think of the money it costs her to do this work; because By the Bay Rescue is not a registered charity, expenses are paid for out of pocket—usually *her* pocket. So why is she so dedicated? She's an ardent advocate for large-breed dogs and seeks to educate potential owners of their needs so that they don't end up with more than they bargained for. "Larger breeds require so much more caution and care than most people know about," LeeAnn says.

But beneath her formal answer is a more personal reason. "I do it for the love of Max and Dakota."

LeeAnn never expected to become a fan of Rottweilers. The breed, developed in Rottweil, Germany, in the 1800s, was intended to be powerful and muscular, with a strong protective instinct. Their original purpose was to drive herds of cattle between farms and butcher, guarding the cattle from thieves along the way. Although the breed almost died out at one point, the Rottweiler is one of the most popular breeds today. Unfortunately, the irresponsible breeding and training that accompany their trendy status have damaged the breed, earning the dogs a reputation for viciousness that doesn't apply to most carefully bred Rottweilers. LeeAnn knows that owning a large, powerful dog is not a responsibility to take lightly. She also knows that in Max and Dakota she got far more back than she ever gave.

Dakota, a well-bred, strapping female puppy, arrived from a reputable breeder in southern Ontario on schedule, just as promised. She grew into a calm, intelligent dog that did everything "by the book." She listened carefully and obeyed commands promptly, displaying caution and reliability.

Max, on the other hand, couldn't have been more different. He was shipped from a breeder in Cleveland, Ohio, and right from the start, he kept LeeAnn on her toes. "Remember the ice storm in Quebec?" LeeAnn asks. "That's when he arrived." With several unexpected flight changes in his itinerary, he never once landed as scheduled. Due to the extreme weather problems, his flight was delayed first in Ottawa, then again in Halifax. In the end, LeeAnn had to hire a customs officer to go pick up the puppy from the airport and drive him home. She heard later that flight attendants were frantically trying to stuff him into his crate on the tarmac because they hadn't had the heart to keep the little guy crated during the flight. He'd flown the entire way snuggling with one attendant or another. By the time they finally reached their destination, he had no intention of going from a warm, soft jacket to a cold plastic crate!

Max grew into a 140-pound tank of a dog with an agenda all of his own. The day that LeeAnn encountered the moose, her dogs' unique combination of attributes—Dakota's intelligence and Max's stubbornness—probably saved her life.

LeeAnn always took precautions when hiking and tracking with the dogs. Moose cows are extremely protective of their young—ready and willing to take on a full-grown black bear if necessary. But when they do not feel threatened, they usually keep to themselves, preferring to melt into the background rather than meet up with humans. In her several years of hiking, LeeAnn had never encountered any moose.

Still, she knew from experience that moose could be unpredictable. Once, as she was driving home from work at about 4:00 a.m., a yearling calf appeared in front of her vehicle. Usually, yearlings aren't so much dangerous as they are disoriented and frightened. Each season when the cows give birth, the previous year's calves are sent out into the world, whether they like it or not. "They're all legs," LeeAnn laughs. "They don't know what to do with themselves." But by their first winter, calves can easily weigh over 200 pounds and are capable of inflicting serious damage to anything perceived as a predator. When LeeAnn saw this particular youngster, she slammed on the brakes, turned off her headlights and hoped he'd make his way out of town. Instead, he fled blindly toward a couple of late-night bar patrons who were staggering down a nearby street. LeeAnn honked her horn to warn them, but they didn't notice, and the calf ran right into them. A moment later, she saw the inebriated twosome sit up and look around as if wondering what had hit them.

Meeting a scared juvenile is one thing. A high-speed collision with a 900-pound adult is another, and wandering moose are a well-known Newfoundland road hazard. But the most dangerous time of year by far is the autumn breeding season or "rut." During this season, bull moose can become very aggressive in their search for cows, attacking other bulls and even humans who have the misfortune to cross their paths.

The day that LeeAnn met her moose, she purposely went out in the afternoon, when moose are least active. As her hike wound to an end, the wind picked up and it started to hail. It was definitely time to head for home. The cracking sounds she heard in the bush came from the area where park officials were clearing a new trail, but LeeAnn knew the workers were gone for the day. Suddenly, Dakota, who was dancing around anxiously, ran to Max, body-slammed him in the shoulder. and took off into the bush. "Dakota flew off in the direction of the sound," recalls LeeAnn, "and my Max, God love him, for the first time ever sat and stayed in one place." That one place happened to be right on LeeAnn's feet.

LeeAnn was frantic to call Dakota back from wherever she'd gone, but Max wasn't about to let her go. "It's the first time she didn't recall to me," she says. "She wasn't listening; I rang the bell and still she wouldn't return." She screamed for Dakota to come back, trying to push Max out of the way so she could run after her other dog, when suddenly she looked up and discovered what the dogs already knew: a moose was charging down the hill directly toward her. And it wasn't just any moose. It was a huge black moose, in full rut and furious.

"This animal was so big, small spruce were falling down around his antlers," says LeeAnn. Behind the moose raced Dakota, nipping at its heels like a herding dog, directing the charge as her German ancestors once did. Dakota seemed to know exactly what she was doing, but LeeAnn was terrified that the moose would turn and aim its deadly hooves or antlers at the dog. She wanted to get Dakota away from the moose, but she couldn't move with the weight of Max against her. Each time she moved, he moved in front of her, blocking her way.

LeeAnn watched the drama unfolding in front of her as if it were happening in slow motion. There was nowhere else for this moose to go but past her. The trail ran alongside the river, and suddenly she realized that Dakota was deliberately herding the moose away from her, toward the water's edge. Persistently, Dakota nipped and barked at the animal's heels, always keeping herself between the moose and her owner.

Finally, Dakota drove the moose down through the rough bush of the embankment, pushing it over the rocky ground. The whole time, LeeAnn was screaming at Max, who steadfastly ignored her. Dakota got the moose down into the water and stayed on the beach until the animal was halfway across the river. Then, to LeeAnn's horror, she saw the moose turn around for another pass. "It didn't want to go across the river, for some reason," she says. This time, Dakota went into the river and swam out until she was within three metres of the moose, barking and making a big racket in the water. Max, knowing LeeAnn was out of danger, went down over the embankment to help Dakota. Upon seeing both of the dogs, the moose decided it wasn't worth the fight and turned toward the other side of the river.

Late that night, LeeAnn heard on the radio that in another part of the province, a man had been gored by a moose in rut, barely escaping with his life. That's when it hit her. "It takes the wind right out of you," she recalls. "If I'd been hiking by myself I'd have been hurt, without a doubt. If the dogs hadn't done what they did, I'd have been face to face with that moose." The two dogs had worked as a team, independent of LeeAnn. Although she'd trained them, they'd known that they had to disregard her commands in order to protect her.

Canine heroes Max (left) and Dakota earned their place on the couch. O'REILLY O'ROTTIES

The next summer, LeeAnn and the dogs encountered another hazard of moose country: bogs. It was a hot July day, and they'd gone down an unfamiliar road, hoping to find some shade. Thinking she could see a little pond ahead that might provide relief from the heat, LeeAnn let the dogs off their leads. Max immediately headed through a patch of scrubby brush in the direction of the water. When LeeAnn called Max to return and he didn't respond, she became worried and sent Dakota to find him.

"She returned in just minutes, grabbed the leash from

my hand and took off barking wildly," says LeeAnn. Dakota pulled and whined anxiously until they pushed through the brush and found Max up to his neck in the quagmire and sinking fast. "I knew there were bogs and that some of them are bottomless," LeeAnn says. "But I thought we were on firm footing."

The famous backwoods bogs can be deadly; some are shallow, while others are so deep that trucks can disappear in a matter of minutes. LeeAnn didn't recognize the danger immediately, but Dakota did. The dog ran between her owner and Max, blocking LeeAnn with her body. She dropped the leash at LeeAnn's feet and then did something the woman had never seen her do: she got down onto her belly and crawled toward Max. LeeAnn followed suit, creeping on her belly until she could reach Max. She attached his lead and then grabbed Dakota by the collar. Together, LeeAnn and Dakota began to pull.

"Within seconds," she says, "I'm up to my armpits in this boggy stuff. Max is still lying there on his side, stuck. Now I'm the one sinking." Dakota lay flat on the ground, distributing her body weight so she wouldn't sink, and dug in her claws. LeeAnn gripped Max's collar in one hand and Dakota's collar in the other and they half crawled, half swam their way to solid ground. "If it wasn't for her thinking," remembers LeeAnn, "I would have gone in, too."

LeeAnn was badly shaken by the incident. Because she hadn't planned to hike the new trail, no one even knew where she'd gone. She and her dogs could have disappeared without a trace. "It changed the way I hiked," she says.

Now, she scouts out her hiking areas and keeps the dogs on leads until she knows it's safe to roam freely. And she always files a "hike plan" with her husband, who was understandably alarmed at her experience. "He told me, 'For God's sake, LeeAnn, tell me where you're going! At least roughly!'"

Wiser for the experiences, LeeAnn continued hiking with Max and Dakota. "What," she often wondered, "would I ever do without them?"

But one night when LeeAnn let the dogs outside, Dakota came back into the house looking distinctly unwell, her body stiff, her head hanging. Panicking, LeeAnn phoned her veterinarian, who guessed that Dakota was reacting to something she'd eaten and would probably be fine by the next day. But the next morning, before LeeAnn could get her to the veterinarian, Dakota took a turn for the worse. LeeAnn was outside the house when she heard her husband screaming at her to hurry in. She dashed back just in time to see Dakota draw her last breath. She gathered the big dog into her arms in disbelief. How could she live without Dakota?

LeeAnn was devastated. How did a perfectly healthy dog become deathly ill seemingly overnight? A veterinary examination on the body gave her the answer: Dakota had a hemangiosarcoma, a large tumour on her spleen. She'd most likely had it for some time without symptoms, until the night it ruptured and she became ill. It was amazing that she lived through the night.

As heartbroken as LeeAnn was, it was even more difficult to watch Max grieve for his friend. Before LeeAnn took Dakota's body away for cremation, she brought Max to the van to let him say goodbye. After LeeAnn returned without her, Max repeatedly sat down next to the van and howled. He searched the house restlessly, looking to LeeAnn as if to say, "Where is she?" He couldn't relax. He lost interest in eating.

Five days after Dakota died, LeeAnn looked at Max and her heart filled with foreboding. She saw something in his eyes that terrified her. Something, she knew not what, was terribly wrong with him. She rushed him to her veterinary clinic in a panic and told them, "He's dying!" They checked him over thoroughly, taking blood samples and X-rays, but everything turned up normal. "They told me he was fine, not to worry," says LeeAnn. "But I knew he was dying. I didn't leave him for a minute."

When Max's appetite continued to flag, LeeAnn had him retested. This time there were some minor changes in his blood results, and the veterinarian diagnosed hemolytic anemia. Although this is a serious illness, it can usually be successfully managed medically. "We thought we had it nailed," remembers LeeAnn. "We could treat him with prednisone and he'd be fine." But secretly she still feared he wasn't going to make it.

LeeAnn is forever grateful for the patience, dedication and expertise of her veterinarians. They understood her grief for Dakota and knew how it drove her fears for Max. They tried to reassure her, but they didn't discount her insistence that something more was wrong. Once again, her instincts were tragically accurate. Max had developed a malignant mast cell tumour, a cancer as deadly as it is difficult to diagnose.

Two weeks to the day after the death of Dakota, Max passed away. In some ways, it was fitting that he died so soon after her. "He never got over her being gone," says LeeAnn. But the loss of both dogs in such a short time hit hard. LeeAnn continues doing her rescue work, more dedicated than ever to the plight of needy dogs. In her car hangs a silver locket containing ashes from both Max and Dakota, a daily reminder to her of the love the dogs gave her. They threw all their vast abilities into doing whatever needed doing; now their memory inspires her to keep doing what needs to be done.

CHAPTER

10

Collies Against
the Odds

IT'S TRAINING DAY ON THE southern Alberta sheep ranch. The gate swings open and as one, the sheep scramble to the far side of the dust-choked corral. They shift nervously from side to side, trying to keep their distance from the mesmerizing eyes of the dogs slinking around them. These dogs, young border collies, don't need training so much as the opportunity to discover and hone the skills lying just beneath the surface. The moment they focus their sharp eyes on the sheep, centuries of breeding click into gear. Marrow-deep instinct stiffens muscles, narrows their gaze and shifts limbs into the predatory crouch that will bend the churning herd to the dogs' will.

All of the border collies in training are doing what

comes naturally. All, that is, except for one; a small black and white puppy cowers outside the gate. More frightened than even the sheep, she refuses to join the other dogs.

If ever a breed of dog was meant to work, it's the border collie. They rank at the top of every canine intelligence test; they excel in obedience matches, agility, flyball and—of course—sheep-herding competitions. But even some border collies have phobias. Some might be scared of lightening or thunder. Others may feel threatened by a broom or a vacuum cleaner.

While a number of phobias are easily explained, others make no human sense whatsoever. Unfortunately, a dog's phobias can cause serious problems for those who live with the animal. Sometimes anti-anxiety drugs help. Desensitization through behaviour-modification techniques can also be effective for many dogs. Some owners simply learn to work around the trigger. But on this busy, sprawling ranch where everyone—human and animal alike—had a job, there was no time to deal with the cowering puppy. For this one little dog named Eve, all the dormant talents in the world didn't compensate for her one vital deficiency: she was a sheepherder who wouldn't herd sheep.

On most ranches, such a situation might be handled with expedient, if reluctant, practicality. But Eve escaped such an end. Unwilling to "dispose" of her, the rancher called the Border Collie Club of Canada and they, in turn, contacted Brenda Kovac and her fiancé, Brent Fukuda, of Calgary,

Alberta. At that time, the two were actively involved in border collie rescue, often providing foster care for dogs awaiting new homes. Brenda, who had rescued her first border collie from the pound 25 years earlier, had known back then that it would only be a matter of time before she got involved in breed rescue officially. "I've always loved dogs," says Brenda, "so it really didn't have to be a border. But I've always been drawn to any collie-type dog."

Even with all the combined rescue experience that Brenda and Brent shared, the timid little Eve presented something of a challenge. At just past one year of age, Eve hadn't had any training or socialization and was terrified of her new world. "I didn't even get a chance to touch her until she'd been with us for a week," Brenda remembers. "She was terrified of everything in the house, right down to the linoleum." Then, Brent showed Eve a ball. Like everything else, this was new to her, but to their relief, it didn't appear to terrify her. Instead, Eve looked interested. "Brent got on all fours, down at her level," says Brenda, "and she woke up and paid attention." The ball was the connection they'd been looking for.

Brenda and Brent began to work with Eve, helping her to get accustomed to life in a home. "We had to train her to do everything," says Brenda. "She wasn't housebroken and she had no manners." It was a huge change for Eve to go from a big, open farm where she spent most of her life surrounded by other dogs, to living in a house in close contact with people. She even balked at leaving the yard, trembling at the sight of the leash. Brenda suspects that Eve's early experiences on the ranch were more traumatic for the sensitive dog's temperament than anyone could have expected. "They had to put her on the leash to drag her into the corral," she says, "and to this day she's scared of sheep."

Knowing Eve as she does now, it makes complete sense to Brenda. Sheep are nervous, simple-minded creatures, and the sounds they make, especially the lambs, are similar to human cries. "Eve picks up on everything," Brenda emphasizes. "The main thing in her life is she doesn't want to upset anyone." For her, the cacophony of frightened animals, and knowing she was the cause, must have been overwhelming. But Brenda's aim wasn't to help Eve overcome her fear of sheep; it was to prepare her for life as a pet in a permanent home. After three months of foster care and constant, gentle training, Eve was ready. Brenda and Brent said goodbye and hoped for the best, but they knew they'd miss the timid collie. They'd grown attached to her gentle presence. "When the dogs find a home, you're happy," Brenda says, "but you're sad, too."

Less than a year later, their paths crossed again, under tragic circumstances. The new owner Eve had quickly grown to love had died suddenly, leaving the dog bereft and homeless yet again. When Brenda and Brent saw her this time, they knew Eve had been through enough. All the progress she'd made was gone. She cowered and shook, afraid of everything, suspecting the worst of the world. They knew Eve needed security, so they decided to make her a permanent member of their family. "Brent had really missed her," says Brenda. "She's had such a hard and difficult life, he just said 'no more.'"

They started over with Eve, slowly regaining her trust. "It took some time for her to come to us again," recalls Brenda. "Eve was looking for her owner, grieving for her." But she settled in gradually and became part of the household, along with Brenda and Brent's two other dogs. Eve even chose her own special place in the living room on the loveseat, next to the window so she could watch passersby.

Brenda spent the next year helping Eve become more comfortable with strangers and new situations. But Brenda suspected that the shy dog needed even more stimulation. She knew from experience that all border collies need to feel useful, so one weekend the following spring, she took Eve to an introductory tracking seminar run by Marcy Wright, a handler certified with the RCMP Civilian Search Dog Association (CSDA). Although tracking work had always intrigued Brenda, she'd never pursued it. "I never thought I could do it," she says, "or that I had a good enough dog." She was just there to expose Eve to something new and let her watch the other dogs. But a change immediately came over Eve. Her eyes lit up; she became alert and focused.

Noting Eve's reaction, Wright and Brenda decided to let her give tracking a try, and Brenda set a scent track. "Our tracking area was a bare field," she explains. "No humans had been in it." Brenda picked out a line about 90 metres long, walked the length of it, set a favourite toy of Eve's down at the end of it, and then left the area without disturbing the line. Next, she took Eve to the beginning of the line, pointed to it and told Eve to "track it." Eve followed the line perfectly! Wright was impressed but figured it was probably a fluke. "So we set another track, a harder one this time," continues Brenda. "It went around a tree, over here, over there." This time, Wright ran alongside, keeping a close eye on Eve as she worked. By the end, Wright knew Eve had something special. "Marcy said it's quite rare for a dog to perform so well, almost by the book," says Brenda. After the seminar, Wright invited Brenda and Eve to train with the CSDA team in Calgary.

But they were coming into the group at a tremendous disadvantage; everyone else was six months ahead of them in their training. And Eve was still Eve. Her fearful nature didn't inspire confidence. "Everyone said 'I don't know about Eve,'" recalls Brenda. "They couldn't even pet her."

Being part of the CSDA isn't a casual commitment; it requires countless volunteer hours of practice. Handlers must undergo rigorous training, learning such skills as first aid, search and rescue fundamentals, global positioning system operations, evidence handling and courtroom demeanour. Civilian dogs are trained to the same tracking standards as the RCMP dogs, with a few exceptions: they are *not* trained to search for drugs or explosives, nor are they trained to be aggressive. In the first year, certification tests require dogs to perform exercises in agility, obedience, finding an article, finding a person and searching a ditch. Dogs are trained to alert their handlers to the presence of human scent in a variety of locations, from wilderness to alleys, ditches and water. Experienced dogs may be trained in the more advanced task of locating human remains.

Brenda and Eve had a lot of work ahead of them. Eve had to learn to make subtle distinctions between commands. "Track it" means to follow a scent trail from start to finish. "Small search" means to look for evidence, while "search" is a general command referring to all other types of searching. It takes an average of a year and a half, but sometimes two or three years, to train a dog to pass the certification tests.

Brenda and Eve worked hard and quickly caught up to the rest of their group, several of whom were preparing to take the certification tests that spring. "We were told, 'You're probably not ready, but give it a try and see what happens,'" says Brenda. So, in April 2002, the pair travelled to Red Deer, Alberta, to see what they could do. The test was a demanding, all-day event. Timid Eve would be required to perform surrounded by strange people in an unknown environment. How would she respond?

Eve gave a stellar performance that day. When she was told to "search," all of her fears and insecurities evaporated. "It was like you'd turned on a light switch," says Brenda. "No matter how shy she was, she was very confident and eager to do this job." In one test activity, two objects are hidden in a field, and the dogs must find them both within 30 minutes. Eve found the first one in eight seconds, and five minutes later she had uncovered the second one. It was a pivotal moment in her career as a civilian search dog. "Ten of us did the testing," says Brenda proudly, "and Eve and I were the only ones that passed!" Eve became the first civilian-owned dog in Calgary to be certified as an RCMP Civilian Search and Rescue Dog. She'd found her niche.

But talent and knowledge are nothing if they aren't used. Shortly after she received her certification, Eve got her first opportunity to try out her skills in an actual search. Residents of an upscale neighbourhood just outside of Edmonton had reported hearing gunshots in the middle of the night. The local police brought in a search dog to look for bullet casings, but they didn't find any, nor did they find anything else that indicated the need for further investigation. The police were satisfied, but the homeowners weren't. They'd heard gunshots and wouldn't rest until they'd received an explanation. At that point, the CSDA was contacted, and Brenda and Eve, as well as others in the group, came to do a search of the area. Fifteen minutes into the search, Eve found something that no one had thought to look for: a spent firecracker. "It was the first indication that it wasn't guns but rather firecrackers that had made the noise," says Brenda. The people in the neighbourhood were satisfied, and the case was closed.

Eve continues to make progress, though her basic personality remains the same: shy and submissive. Still, she's come a long way—from the sheep dog who was afraid of sheep to a highly valued member of the Civilian Search Dog Association.

Eve's a lucky dog, but Brenda and Brent feel the good fortune is theirs. They love having her in their lives. Recently, Brenda was invited to do a demonstration with Eve at the world-famous Calgary Stampede. Once more, Eve will be surrounded by the sights and sounds of farm animals, even sheep. She probably won't like it, but she's got more important things to think about these days. "We're all pretty excited," says Brenda proudly. "This little girl is taking us on all sorts of adventures."

* * *

In Baltimore, Maryland, a newborn collie caused her breeder to look on with dismay as the pup nuzzled her mother sleepily. The puppy's two brothers appeared to be developing normally, but something was wrong with this little female. Smaller than usual, she had a slight head tilt and something looked different about her face. At three weeks of age, when the puppy's eyes still hadn't opened, the breeder took her to the veterinarian. The news wasn't good: the puppy had a condition described as "bilateral agenesis of eyes." Through a fluke of nature, this little female had been born without eyes.

Naturally, the breeder was distressed. Nothing like this

had ever cropped up in her bloodline before. Her dogs were healthy show champions; she'd even bred one two-time winner of the National Specialty. Distraught, she turned to her computer and posted a message on an Internet newsgroup for collie owners. What should she do?

When Jana Lashmit, also of Baltimore, logged on to the collie-owner forum, it was more out of habit than interest. The recent death of her own collie left her grieving and unable to participate with her usual enthusiasm. "I read it every day, but after Parker passed away, I was ready to quit the collie list," she says, "except my 'unsubscribe message' had an error so I was still getting mail." The message about the puppy without eyes caught her attention. When other forum members suggested euthanasia, Jana decided to post her own message. She wanted to meet the puppy herself.

"I didn't want another collie," she insists, "but Bonnie was something special. She was as spunky and playful as any eight-week-old."

Jana took Bonnie home with her. Then she began the long task of teaching a blind dog to live in a sighted world. "Training her wasn't easy at first," she admits. The open spaces beyond the comfortable walls of the house overwhelmed Bonnie. When carried outdoors, she flopped to the ground and refused to move. Nothing could entice her to do so much as lift her head.

Jana began to wonder if she would ever be able to go for real walks with Bonnie. "Finally," she says, "on a nice warm day in April when Bonnie was three and a half months old, I just outwaited her." She spread a blanket out in the sun and sat down beside Bonnie, patiently waiting for the puppy to gain enough courage to sit up. When Bonnie finally did, Jana praised her lavishly, then rewarded her by taking her back inside her beloved home. The ice was broken. Gently, Jana continued to push Bonnie to explore further. Every tentative venture was followed by a reassuring trip home.

Jana decided that Bonnie needed to be treated like any other puppy. Housetraining followed, as well as learning to accept a leash. Puppy classes and regular obedience training came soon after. Bonnie was quickly turning into a normal dog—almost. "She even chased ducks," remembers Jana. "When she heard them quack, she'd weave her head back and forth like a satellite dish, and when she realized where they were, she'd run toward them at top speed, head still tipped at an angle."

Jana knew that socialization would be particularly important for her shy, blind collie, so she made sure Bonnie was exposed to plenty of new situations. Jana's two jobs—one at a veterinary hospital and one at a pet store—allowed her to bring Bonnie to work with her every day. That way, Bonnie could grow accustomed to meeting strangers. The little dog's personality blossomed. Before long, Bonnie had passed her Canine Good Citizen test, a practical, non-competitive evaluation meant to improve manners. As well, she became a certified "therapy dog," able to do hospital and nursing-home visitations. Both tests are a wonderful way for ordinary dogs to become better members of society. "Mixed breeds are also allowed to earn them," explains Jana, "but they aren't recorded on a dog's pedigree like obedience or agility would be."

Still, Jana worried that this would be the extent of Bonnie's achievements. She knew that Bonnie's family tree contained many talented canines, athletes titled in sports that were simply beyond the reach of a blind dog. Bonnie clearly had the necessary intelligence, as well as the desire to work, but the typical collie sports—obedience, agility and herding—weren't options. "It didn't seem fair," says Jana, "that she should always be an outsider."

So Jana looked into other activities. "Again, the Internet came to the rescue!" she says. In the spring of 2001, she discovered draft work, a sport dominated by large dogs specifically bred for the task of hauling carts. Jana didn't care whether or not Bonnie would win any competitions; she only wanted Bonnie to have something she could enjoy participating in. "I ordered a harness right away and an adapter kit that transforms a child's wagon into a dog-powered vehicle," Jana says. To her surprise, Bonnie took to draft work immediately. Before the first day ended, the dog was happily pulling the wagon behind her, doing wide circles around the yard.

After less than a week, Bonnie was doing so well that Jana decided to enter her in a draft-dog competition put on by the American Rottweiler Club. The pair intensified their training. The day of the event, as Jana looked at the more than 20 dogs entered, she silently berated herself. Everywhere she turned, there were big, powerful cart-pullers: Rottweilers, as well as a Bernese mountain dog, a Swiss mountain dog and a Leonberger. What had she been thinking? Bonnie was the only "non-traditional" draft dog there; the only dog who weighed less than her cart—not to mention the only dog without eyes!

Even the sopping grass surface was different from the dry earth or pavement they'd practised on at home. Nevertheless, the duo had entered the competition, and they would participate. After all, *Bonnie* didn't feel nervous or discouraged. As soon as their turn came, Jana's fears evaporated. "She threw herself into the harness and pulled as well as always," says Jana, "slow and steady." That day, Bonnie did herself proud: of all the dogs entered, she finished in second place with a score of 98 out of a possible 100 points.

Jana could see that Bonnie enjoyed the challenge. Next, they set out to train for the Draft Dog test put on by the Saint Bernard Club of America. This time it wasn't quite as easy; during the first test, the cart caught on a turn. However, on the second try, Bonnie passed—the only dog out of seven to succeed. Jana now knew that Bonnie could hold her own—but was she good enough to earn an official title from the American Kennel Club? They'd have to find out.

That's when Jana discovered that official regulations do not permit blind dogs to compete in AKC-sanctioned events.

Jana Lashmit and Bonnie get ready to take the Draft Dog test.
DOROTHY HANSEN

"I was a little disappointed, but not really surprised," says Jana. She and Bonnie would have to be content with participating in the local clubs that accepted Bonnie's disability.

Or would they? On a whim, she telephoned the central office of the Canadian Kennel Club to see if, by any chance, they might allow blind dogs to compete. "The nice young man I asked just paused a moment, then said, 'Well, I don't see why not!'" Jana remembers. "Then he checked the rules just to be sure." Bonnie, he told her, was welcome to compete for titles in CKC-sanctioned events, just like any other dog.

Jana was thrilled. "I love the idea of Bonnie competing on equal footing with 'normal' dogs," she says. That autumn, she and Bonnie packed for the trip up north, crossing the border into Ontario, where Bonnie's blindness wasn't a barrier. "It's about a 12-hour drive every time I go up to Canada to compete," says Jana, "but it's a pretty drive, straight up through rural Pennsylvania and New York, and past Niagara Falls." In October 2002, after much work, Bonnie the blind collie received her official Draft Dog title, as bestowed by the Canadian Kennel Club.

Jana and Bonnie are currently planning to take the CKC Draft Dog Excellent test, but meanwhile, Jana keeps Bonnie busy with her other jobs. With a group called Fidos for Freedom, they continue their regular pet visitation therapy to the sick and elderly. Bonnie also works as a "reading dog" with Dogs Educating and Assisting Readers (DEAR). "We go to libraries with 6 to 10 other dog/handler teams and have third-graders come and read to the dogs," she says. "Bonnie has a little green cape and her own ID tag to wear on her visits." These dogs, who listen without judging or correcting, make great reading partners for the children, and Bonnie is as non-threatening as they come.

Bonnie has come a long way from the frightened puppy who once wouldn't even lift her head off the ground. She's handicapped, but she doesn't know it. All she knows is that when Jana asks her to do a task, it must be important, so she does it. It's her job.

CHAPTER

11

The Gift of Courage

MARK WAS ABOUT 11 YEARS OLD, skinny and slouching, when he and his mom first brought Mojo into the clinic where I worked. Baggy clothes dwarfed the boy's small frame, and under a battered baseball hat, his challenging blue eyes glared at the world. Clearly, we had to earn Mark's trust before we could do anything with his dog. Mojo was around nine then, old for a black Labrador retriever, but not too old to still have fun. But recently it seemed that Mojo had lost all his spunk.

Mark listened intently as the doctor examined his dog and answered his questions. The boy nervously brushed back wisps of blond hair that escaped the hat onto his furrowed brow.

"Mojo's going to be okay, isn't he?" he blurted as the doctor turned to leave. There were no guarantees, and when the blood work came back, the doctor's suspicions were confirmed. Mojo had liver and kidney disease, progressive and ultimately fatal. With care, he could live comfortably for a while, but he'd need special food, regular checkups and medications. The doctor and I knew finances were a struggle, but the moment euthanasia was suggested, Mark's mom broke in. "We're not putting Mojo to sleep." Quickly and quietly they paid their bill and gently led their old dog out to the car without a backward glance.

We didn't hear from them for a few weeks, but then one day, there they were. Mojo had lost weight. He'd been sick, they said, and he seemed listless. As I led Mojo back to the treatment room for some IV fluid therapy, Mark's little body blocked the way. "I have to go with him—he needs me," the boy said firmly. I wasn't sure how Mark would handle the sight of needles and blood, but there didn't seem any point in arguing. And indeed, Mark handled it all as if he'd seen it a million times before.

"Oh, you're such a brave old guy, Mojo," Mark murmured as the catheter slipped into Mojo's vein. We seldom had a more cooperative patient. Mojo only moved his head slightly during uncomfortable procedures, as if to remind us that he was still there. He seemed to take strength from the small, white hand that continually moved in reassurance over his grizzled throat.

This became a pattern. We'd get Mojo stabilized somewhat, send him home, he'd get sick again, and they'd be back. Always, Mark was there, throwing out questions and reminders to be careful, but mostly encouraging his old pal. I worried that Mark found it too difficult to watch, but any hint that maybe he'd rather wait outside was flatly rejected. Mojo needed him.

I approached Mark's mom one day, while Mark and Mojo were in the other room. "You know Mojo's condition is getting worse. Have you thought any more about how far you want to go with treatment? It looks like Mark is really having a hard time with all this."

Mark's mom hesitated a moment before leaning forward and speaking in a low, intense voice, "We've had Mojo since Mark was a baby. They've grown up together, and Mark loves him beyond all reason. But that's not all."

She took a deep breath and looked away momentarily, "Two years ago, Mark was diagnosed with leukemia. He's been fighting it, and they tell us he has a good chance of recovering completely. But he never talks about it. He goes for tests and treatments as if it's happening to someone else, as if it's not real. But about Mojo, he can ask questions. It's important to Mark, so as long as he wants to, we'll keep on fighting for Mojo."

Over the next few weeks we saw a lot of the quiet little trio. Mark's abrupt questions and observations, once slightly annoying, now had a new poignancy, and we explained at length every procedure as it was happening. We wondered how long Mojo could carry on. A more stoic and good-natured patient was seldom seen, but the Labrador was so terribly thin and weak now. All of us at the clinic really worried about how Mark would handle the inevitable.

Finally, the day came when Mojo collapsed before his scheduled appointment. It was a Saturday when they rushed him in, and the waiting room was packed. We carried Mojo into the back room and settled him on some thick blankets, with Mark at his side as usual. I left to get some supplies, and when I re-entered the room a few moments later I was shocked to see Mark standing at the window, fists jammed into his armpits, tears streaming down his face. I backed out of the room noiselessly, not wanting to disturb him. He'd been so brave up until now. Later, when we returned, he was kneeling, dry-eyed once more, at Mojo's side. His mom sat down beside him and squeezed his shoulders. "How are you guys doing?" she asked softly.

"Mom," he said, ignoring her question, "Mojo's dying, isn't he?"

"Oh, honey . . . ," her voice broke, and Mark continued as if she hadn't spoken.

"I mean, the fluids and the pills, they're just not going to help anymore, are they?" He looked to us for confirmation. "Then I think," he swallowed hard, "I think we should put him to sleep."

True to form, Mark stayed with Mojo until the end. He

asked questions to satisfy himself that it truly was best for Mojo, and that there would be no pain or fear for his old friend. Over and over again he smoothed the glossy head, until it faded onto his knee for the last time. As Mark felt the last breath leave Mojo's thin ribs and watched the light dim in the kind brown eyes, he seemed to forget about the rest of us. Crying openly, he bent himself over Mojo's still form and slowly removed his cap. With a jolt, I recognized the effects of chemotherapy, so harsh against such a young face. We left him to his grief.

Mark never told us anything about his illness, or his own feelings throughout Mojo's ordeal, but when his mom called months later to ask some questions about a puppy she was considering buying, I asked her how he was doing.

"You know," she said, "it was a terrible time for him, but since Mojo's death, Mark has begun talking about his own condition, asking questions and trying to learn more about it. I think that dealing with Mojo when the dog was so sick gave Mark strength to fight for himself and courage to face his own pain."

I always thought Mark was being brave for Mojo, but when I remember those calm, trusting eyes and gently wagging tail that never failed no matter how bad he felt, I think maybe Mojo was being brave for Mark.

Bibliography

Alderton, David. *Eyewitness Handbooks: Dogs.* Ontario: Stoddart Publishing Co. Ltd., 1993.

Budiansky, Stephen. *The Truth About Dogs.* New York: Penguin Putnam Inc., 2000.

Owens, Carrie. *Working Dogs.* Rocklin: Prima Publishing, 1999.

Sheldrake, Rupert. *Dogs That Know When Their Owners Are Coming Home.* New York: Three Rivers Press, 1999.

Slowik, Teresa. *The Ultimate Dog Quiz Book.* New York: Howell Book House, 1996.

Acknowledgements

The author extends her sincere thanks to all the dog enthusiasts who generously shared their stories for this book: Corporal Terry Barter and Corporal Rick Chaulk of the RCMP Police Dog Service, Marsha Armstrong, Judi Snowdon, Ros Scott, Heather MacLeod, Brenda Kovac, Jana Lashmit, Denise Castonguay, LeeAnn O'Reilly and Jean Little, who all love their dogs dearly. Your patience and helpful comments were much appreciated!

Also, I'd like to thank my biggest fans: Stephanie, Andrea and Megan, for reading my stories and making their own lunches, and Ray, for cheerfully taking the smaller office.

About the Author

Roxanne Willems Snopek has been writing professionally for two decades and is the author of eight books and more than 150 articles. Her non-fiction has appeared in a wide variety of publications, from the *Vancouver Sun* and *Reader's Digest* to newsletters for Duke, Cornell and Tufts universities. In 2006, her novel *Targets of Affection* was published by Cormorant Books. Written under the name RG Willems, it is the first of a new mystery series dealing with the human-animal bond. Short fiction by Roxanne is included in the anthologies *Half in the Sun* (Ronsdale Press, Elsie K. Neufeld, ed.) and *Blood on the Holly* (Baskerville Books, Caro Soles, ed.). Roxanne and her family live in British Columbia, where she is currently at work on her next book.

More Amazing Stories by Roxanne Willems Snopek

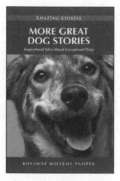

More Great Dog Stories
Inspirational Tales About Exceptional Dogs

(ISBN 978-1-894974-57-8)

Here are tales of people who turned around the lives of their dogs, and dogs who turned around the lives of their people. A retired greyhound named Blaster learns about life beyond the racetrack. A service dog named Blue restores independence to his quadriplegic owner. Dog lovers of all ages will be inspired and moved by these and other true stories.

Great Cat Stories
Memorable Tales of Remarkable Cats

(ISBN 978-1-926613-96-3)

These inspiring stories explore the loving relationship between exceptional cats and their people. A woman devotes herself to caring for feral cats on the cold Saskatoon streets. A clever cat becomes a famous columnist, with just a little help from his writer-owner. From cats that console the ailing to cats that survive against all odds, these memorable felines will warm the hearts of all animal lovers.

Visit heritagehouse.ca to see the entire list of books in this series.